Testing and Securing Web Applications

Testing and Securing Web Applications

By Ravi Das
and Greg Johnson

CRC Press
Taylor & Francis Group
Boca Raton London New York

CRC Press is an imprint of the
Taylor & Francis Group, an **informa** business

AN AUERBACH BOOK

First edition published 2020
by CRC Press
6000 Broken Sound Parkway NW, Suite 300, Boca Raton, FL 33487-2742
and by CRC Press
2 Park Square, Milton Park, Abingdon, Oxon, OX14 4RN

© 2021 Taylor & Francis Group, LLC
CRC Press is an imprint of Taylor & Francis Group, LLC

ISBN: 978-0-367-33375-1 (pbk)
ISBN: 978-1-003-08121-0 (ebk)

Typeset in Adobe Garamond
by Cenveo® Publisher Services

I dedicate this book to my Lord and Savior, Jesus Christ,
the ultimate Creator of the universe we live in, and to my
parents, Dr. Gopal D. Das and Mrs. Kunda G. Das.

I also dedicate this book to my three beloved cats, Libby, Kelly, and Cali.

Contents

Acknowledgments

I would like to thank John Wyzalek, our editor, for his guidance to the completion of this book. Many special thanks go to Greg Johnson, co-author, and David Pearson, contributor.

Ravi Das

As my friend Ravi Das will attest, writing a book is a painstaking labor of love which is only accomplished by the love, support, and assistance of many. The phrase, "It takes a village" is so true here. There are many who played a role and without whom this work would not have come about.

First and foremost, the majority of the credit goes to my supportive family, particularly my wife Kelly of 35 years who has supported me in *so many* endeavors – those that failed as well as those that didn't – and who rarely complains about anything. Nobody's perfect, but I have to say she's pretty darn close!

Next, this work couldn't possibly have materialized without Curt Jeppson, dear friend and colleague of many years, consultant, and VP of engineering for Webcheck Security, as well as his own consultancy, Cyrilliant. Curt is brilliant, honest, kind, a hard worker, willing, and oh, did I say brilliant? It's easy to build a technology business when you're surrounded by people like Curt, without whom my current success in business would be nil.

Significant gratitude goes to Secuvant Security for the support and encouragement of my dear colleagues, EVP and advisor Jeff Smith, and CEO Ryan Layton, and also to the prolific SOC manager and cyclist, Eric Peterson, along with the brilliance of senior analyst, Chris Signorino. You guys are smart, cooperative, and it's no wonder Secuvant is so successful with you two leading the SOC.

Finally, nothing happens in life without many doors and windows having been opened by the divine. I am thankful to a loving Heavenly Father who really is there, who hears and answers prayers, and who blesses me with so many undeserved opportunities and blessings.

Greg Johnson

About the Authors

Ravi Das is a business development specialist for the AST Cybersecurity Group, Inc., a leading cybersecurity content firm located in the greater Chicago area. Ravi holds a Master of Science degree in agribusiness economics (thesis in international trade) and a Master of Business Administration in management information systems.

Ravi has authored five books, with two more upcoming ones on artificial intelligence in cybersecurity and cybersecurity risk and its impact on cybersecurity insurance policies.

Greg Johnson is the CEO of a world-class penetration test company, Webcheck Security. Greg started Webcheck Security after working with several executive teams and serving a long sales and management career with technology companies such as WordPerfect/Novell, SecurityMetrics, A-LIGN, and Secuvant Security. A BYU graduate, Greg began his career in the days of 64k, 5.25" floppy drives and Mac 128k's. As the industry evolved, he moved into the cyber arena and provided his clients with solutions surrounding compliance, digital forensics, data breach, and response, and in 2016 earned his PCI Professional (PCIP) designation.

In several VP of Business Development roles, Greg consulted, guided, and educated clients in compliance guidelines and certifications for standards such as:

- PCI
- HIPAA
- ISO 27001
- NIST
- SOC 1 and SOC 2
- GDPR/CCPA
- FedRAMP

When Greg is not providing cyber solutions for his clients, he can be found spending time with his amazing wife Kelly, playing with his grandchildren, or rehearsing or performing with the world-renowned Tabernacle Choir on Temple Square.

Having used Wireshark ever since it was Ethereal, **David Pearson** has been analyzing network traffic for well over a decade. He has spent the majority of his professional career understanding how networks and applications work. David holds computer security degrees from the Rochester Institute of Technology (BS) and Carnegie Mellon University (MS).

Chapter 1

Network Security

Introduction

Everybody remembers at the 1990s quite well. The stock market was at an all-time high back then, and jobs were plentiful. I even remember the comment that one recruiter made: "If this candidate can even breathe, he is hired." Those were good times for sure. But probably the one thing that will be remembered the most is the era of the .com businesses. It seemed that for any new idea that would pop up, it had to be branded as such.

Of course, the domain extension was also quite popular. In fact, during that time frame, this domain extension could easily fetch $20,000 or more if the actual domain name was in huge demand. It seemed like venture capitalists and angel investors were literally pumping in money into newly founded companies when they didn't even have a business plan or even a business model. If it had a .com in its name, it was well-funded, and no further questions were asked. Because of this, even the NASDAQ reached record new highs. Also, who could forget that famous slogan by Sun Microsystems: "We're the dot in .com"? There were other marketing advertisements like this, and all of the tech companies were riding on a literal high.

For example, the tech giants like Microsoft, Cisco, Adobe, and Oracle all prospered greatly. With Microsoft, all of their software platforms saw a huge uptick, especially their Exchange, Office, and SQL Server product lines. Even their certifications were in huge demand, most notably the Microsoft Certified Systems Engineer (MCSE).

Cisco benefitted primarily from their network offerings, Adobe was most noted (and still is) for their Portable Data File (PDF) structure, and Oracle was probably the most widely used and deployed database for all sorts of software applications. The .com boom also gave birth to a new concept: Rather than having to go to a brick-and-mortar store to buy products and services, one could now purchase these easily via online commerce.

Of course, this concept was still in its infancy, and it was nothing like to the point where it is today, where you see some of the giants of the retail industry having the largest e-commerce storefronts ever imagined. A prime example of this is that of Walmart, Costco, Ace Hardware, etc. The primary advantages of this became quite obvious to the customer.

As mentioned, first, the customer did not have to waste time traveling to a store to purchase the products that they needed. With just a few simple clicks of the mouse, they could select whatever they chose and enter in the credit card information. Within just a matter of minutes, the customer would be checked out, and there was no waiting in line at the checkout lane. This would become the second primary advantage of online shopping.

The third primary advantage that would be realized from these online stores would be that these products could be delivered straight to the doors of the customer that purchased them. There was no need to carry heavy and large boxes in shopping carts to trunks of their cars, in just a matter of days, they would all appear on the doorstep.

The fourth advantage of the online store as it evolved was the products that were purchased could be sent directly to another recipient. For example, this became a huge boon during the holiday season. Once again, rather than having to fight in checkout lines during the last-minute Christmas shopping, the products (or gifts) that were purchased online could be sent to the recipient directly, even completely gift wrapped. So yes, the birth of the online store, or as it would eventually become known, electronic commerce (or simply just e-commerce), would grow to become a powerful asset to the marketing tools of any retailer, whether it was the largest of the large Fortune 500 or all the way down to the smallest of the mom-and-pop stores.

But keep in mind that these e-commerce storefronts were quite simple in design from a technical perspective. Simply put, while they could handle a large volume of shopping and financial transactions, they were nothing at all like how they are today.

These e-commerce sites had literally just a simple front end, which was what the end user would see. This included pictures and pricing of the various product lines, as well as any downloadable brochures or catalogs. Then there was the back end, which was essentially the database. This was where either SQL Server or an Oracle type of database was designed, implemented, and made use of.

Essentially, these databases would contain the personally identifiable information (PII) of the customer, their transaction history, and, if applicable, even their respective credit card and/or banking information so that the customer would not have to repeatedly enter this each and every time they visited an e-commerce site. Back then, these applications were still small enough in nature and did not occupy a good chunk of an organization's entire information technology (IT) infrastructure.

Also the processing power and the bandwidth that were required were well lower than what is required today. In addition, these various e-commerce sites were referred to as "web applications." After all, they were still applications residing on a server somewhere (whether it was on-premises or hosted through a cloud provider) and could only be accessed through an Internet connection (for example, back then, it was either a dial-up modem or Ethernet) – thus, the term "web" became quite applicable as well.

But today's web applications (or "apps" for short) have become both exponentially and gargantuanly complex in nature. For example, literally millions of business transactions can take place within a matter of just a few seconds, and the database size has exploded in terms of the capacity of data and information that it can store. This is in part due to the fact that today, a business can use the tools of data warehousing and even big data not only to track the buying trends of customers today but even predict their future buying patterns using the tools of artificial intelligence (AI) and machine learning (ML).

The web applications today have become so sophisticated that they can even create and customize an automatic shopping experience for each customer every time they visit. For example, if a customer likes products in the XYZ category, then the e-commerce site will advertise not only the products in that category but related ones as well, and even offer various coupons and discounts – some are even delivered straight to the customer's smartphone.

It should also be noted that the days of using a traditional computer to launch and view these kinds of web applications are pretty much a thing of the past; everything is now delivered straight to the smartphone or wireless device, which requires much further demands in terms of a user experience and user interface (also known as UI/UX) of the design and development of a particular web application.

Because of all of this, web applications now occupy a much larger space within the IT infrastructure of a business or a corporation. They simply just don't touch a front end or a back end; today's web apps affect just about every corner of it. Keep in mind that back in the late 1990s as these e-commerce started to evolve, nobody really paid too much attention to a topic that has become critical today: cybersecurity.

For example, the issues of Bitcoin, cryptojacking, ransomware, phishing, business email compromise (BEC), data leaks, data hacks, etc., were simply not heard of or even conceived of back then. True, there were other cyberattacks that were known, such as the traditional Trojan horses and SQL injection attacks, but they did not precipitate to the level of gravity that we know today.

Back then, if an e-commerce site simply had Secure Sockets Layer (SSL) installed, that was good enough. But as mentioned, today's web apps have become crazy complex, which has made them a prime target for the sophisticated cyberattacker of today. As a result of all this, the web apps of today have to be literally tested from the inside out in terms of security before they can be deployed and launched to the public for business transactions to occur.

That is the primary objective of this book – to address those specific areas that have to be tested before a web app can be considered and deemed to be 100% secure. As mentioned, since the web apps of today occupy a much larger space with regard to the IT infrastructure, the number of areas that have to be tested have also increased greatly as well.

In this regard, specifically, five key areas need to be targeted:

1. Network Security:
   This encompasses the various network components that are involved in order for the end user to access the particular web app from the server where it is stored to where it is being transmitted to, whether it is a physical computer itself or a wireless device (such as a smartphone).
2. Cryptography:
   This area includes not only securing the lines of network communications between the server upon which the web app is stored and from where it is accessed from but also ensuring that all PII (most notably the financial information that is being used, such as credit card numbers) that is stored remains in a ciphertext format and that its integrity remains intact while in transmission.
3. Penetration Testing:
   This involves literally breaking apart a web app from the external environment and going inside of it in order to discover all weaknesses and vulnerabilities and making sure that they are patched before the actual web app is launched into a production state of operation.
4. Threat Hunting:
   This is the same as penetration testing, but instead this involves completely breaking down a web app from the internal environment to the external one in order to discover all security holes and gaps.
5. The Dark Web:
   This is that part of the Internet that is not openly visible to the public. As its name implies, this is the "sinister" part of the Internet, and in fact, where much of the PII that is hijacked from a web app cyberattack is sold to other cyberattackers in order to launch more covert and damaging threats to a potential victim, such as that on the Internet.

Since this first chapter deals with network security, obviously, its major component is that of the Internet. Thus, it is imperative to take a chronological examination of the evolution of the Internet and how it is used to connect to a particular web app.

A Chronological History of the Internet

As mentioned in the last section, the Internet is the backbone for any web application, meaning this is the main method in which an end user can access a particular web application they wish to go to. When one types in a domain or uniform resource locator (URL), it takes just a matter of a few seconds for the web application to appear. But the activity that takes place in the background that makes this all possible is quite complex and will be further examined later on in this chapter.

But contrary to popular belief, the Internet did not start in the 1990s. Rather, it dates as far back as the 1960s, with the creation of APRANET. Here is a detailed timeline:

1965:
> Two computers at the MIT Lincoln Lab communicate with one another using packet-switching technology.

1968:
> Beranek and Newman, Inc. (BBN) unveil the final version of the Interface Message Processor (IMP) specifications. The work on ARPANET now starts.

1969:
> On October 29, UCLA's Network Measurement Center, the Stanford Research Institute (SRI), University of California-Santa Barbara, and University of Utah install various network nodes. The first message is "LO," which was an attempt by student Charles Kline to "LOGIN" to the SRI computer from the university. However, the message failed because the SRI system crashed.

1972:
> BBN's Ray Tomlinson introduces network email. The Internetworking Working Group (INWG) forms to address the need for establishing standard email protocols.

1973:
> Global networking becomes a reality as the University College of London (England) and the Royal Radar Establishment (Norway) connect to the ARPANET. The term Internet is now born.

1974:
> The first Internet service provider (ISP) comes into being with the introduction of a commercial version of ARPANET known as Telnet.

1974:
> Vinton Cerf and Bob Kahn (publish "A Protocol for Packet Network Interconnection," which details the design of Transmission Control Protocol [TCP]).

1979:

USENET forms to host news and discussion groups.

1981:

The National Science Foundation (NSF) provides a grant to establish the Computer Science Network (CSNET) to provide networking services to university-based computer scientists.

1982:

TCP and Internet Protocol (IP), as the protocol suite commonly known as TCP/IP, emerge as the main protocol for ARPANET. TCP/IP remains the standard protocol for the Internet.

1983:

The Domain Name System (DNS) establishes the domain extensions of .edu, .gov, .com, .mil, .org, .net, and .int system for naming websites.

1985:

Symbolics.com, the website for Symbolics Computer Corporation in Massachusetts, becomes the first registered domain.

1986:

The NSF's NSFNET goes online to connected supercomputer centers at 56,000 bits per second – the speed of a typical dial-up computer modem. The NSFNET was essentially a network of networks that connected academic users along with ARPANET.

1987:

The number of server hosts on the Internet exceeds 20,000. Cisco ships its first router.

1989:

World.std.com becomes the first commercial provider of dial-up access to the Internet.

1990:

Tim Berners-Lee, a scientist at CERN, the European Organization for Nuclear Research, develops Hypertext Markup Language (HTML).

1991:

CERN introduces the World Wide Web to the public for the very first time.

1992:

The first audio and video are downloaded over the Internet. The phrase "surfing the Internet" is now born.

1993:

The White House and United Nations go online.

1994:

Netscape Communications is born. Microsoft creates a web browser for Windows 95, known as "Internet Explorer."

1995:

CompuServe, America Online, and Prodigy begin to provide the first Internet access.

1996:

A 3D animation dubbed "The Dancing Baby" becomes the first video online to go viral.

1998:

The Google search engine is born.

IP version 6 is introduced to allow for future growth of Internet addresses. The current most widely used protocol is version 4. IPv4 uses 32-bit addresses, allowing for 4.3 billion unique addresses; IPv6, with 128-bit addresses, will allow 3.4 × 1038 unique addresses or 340 trillion trillion trillion.

1999:

Peer-to-peer file sharing is born with the launch of Napster.

2000:

The first cyberattack is launched, as Yahoo! and eBay are hit by a large-scale distributed denial of service (DDoS) attack.

2003:

The SQL Slammer worm is launched and spreads itself worldwide in just 10 minutes.

The blog publishing platform WordPress is launched.

2004:

Facebook goes online, and the era of social networking is now launched.

2005:

YouTube is launched.

2006:

Twitter is officially launched.

2010:

The social media sites Pinterest and Instagram are launched.

2013:

Fifty-one percent of U.S. adults report that they bank online, according to a survey conducted by the Pew Research Center.

2015:

Instagram, the photo-sharing site, reaches 400 million users, outpacing Twitter, which would go on to reach 316 million users by the middle of the same year.

2016:

The first virtual personal assistants (VPAs) are launched, with Google's Alexa, Siri from Apple, and Cortana from Microsoft.

The Evolution of Web Applications

Now that we have reviewed what the evolution of the Internet looks like, it is equally important to provide some background into the history of the evolution of web applications, which is covered in this section.

A lot of web apps now demand some degree of end-user interaction. In many instances, this simply involves inputting some data, primarily in the way of a contact form. For example, most static sites include the following line of code when creating their contact page:

```
<form name="indexform" action="/cgi-bin/password.cgi"
method="POST">
```

In the case of a data validation error, this meant responding with the same form page. Because Hypertext Transfer Protocol (HTTP) is stateless, the values that the end user entered would be lost. A common solution for this was to populate the data input into the value attributes of the form fields when constructing the response. As a result, when the user loaded the form the first time, a given input might look like this:

```
<input name="email" type="text" value="" />
```

The end user would then fill out the form and include a business or personal email address. They would the reenter the information, press Submit, and if there was some sort of data validation error, the form would then be re-created with the following:

```
<input name="email" type="text" value="mic@professionallyevil.
com" />
```

This approach was used for more than 10 years, even through the usage of web domain-specific languages like PHP and the classic ASP.

In some cases, the HTML responses were constructed with simple concatenation, but as technologies progressed, often they used inline code:

```
<input name="email" type="text" value="<?php echo emailAddr
?>" />
```

But there was a big security problem with this. For example, the emailAddr of [mic" onclick="alert(1);] would be inlined as follows (square brackets are only included to delineate the user-supplied input):

```
<input name="email" type="text" value="[mic" onclick=
"alert(1);]">
```

Of course, this could be made safe with input sanitization and/or output encoding, but the primary caveat was that the developer had to remember to implement this kind of syntax in each and every location where it was required in the source code that powered the web application.

This was one factor, but certainly not the only one, that catalyzed the move toward server-side web-specific templates such as ASP.NET WebForms and Java Server Pages (JSP):

```
<asp:TextBox id="emailTextbox" Text="mic@secureideas.com"
runat="server" />
```

As web applications further evolved, especially on the client side, there was the controller, which handled logic related to presentation, for example, event handlers for user interactions such as button clicks.

There was also a viewmodel, the JavaScript object with a two-way binding to the view, which was generally a template or partial template that was rendered on the client side. The two-way binding part, meaning that if the viewmodel is a JavaScript object, looks like this in terms of code:

```
var user = {
userId: 1,
name: 'mic',
email: 'mic@professionallyevil.com'
};
```

This source would then be bound to a contact form, which resembled this:

```
<form>
<input type="hidden" name="id" value="{{userId}}" />
Username: <input type="text" name="username" value="{{name}}" />
Email: <input type="text" name="email" value="{{email}}" />
<button name="save" />
</form>
```

As of today, the three most popular front-end frameworks are React, Vue, and Angular. The general trend today in web application development is to build UIs and UXs as self-contained components, often with hierarchical nesting.

Here is a more detailed history with regard to the evolution of the specific technologies and tools that are used in creating web applications today:

1990:
   HTML is launched.
1993:
   Table-based websites are born. They offer a better content arrangement and navigation style.
1994:
   The World Wide Web Consortium (W3C) is born in an effort to create a common set of best standards.

1996:

Cascading Style Sheets (CSS) and Macromedia (eventually bought by Adobe) are launched.

1997:

HTML Version 4.0 comes out.

1998:

CSS3 and the Hypertext Preprocessor (PHP) are launched.

2000:

The usage of web content editors and content management systems are born.

In this regard, the design components are actually specified in the CSS source code rather than in the HTML itself.

2001–2002:

In a major move for web application development, the navigation bars start to move to the top of websites and drop-down menus become the de facto standard.

2003:

WordPress (a content management system) officially launches.

JavaScript is now used for animation purposes without using Flash.

2005:

Git (a version control system for source code development) is born, and web applications now start to move to smartphones.

2006:

jQuery (a JavaScript library) is launched.

2008:

For web application appearance, thin and tall layouts are preferred over wide and short layouts.

2009:

Node.js (which is an open-source server environment) is released.

2010:

Angular JS (a structural framework for building dynamic web applications) is launched.

NPM (Node Package Manager, an online repository for the publishing of open-source Node.js projects) is launched.

The use of WordPress-based plugins and themes gains widespread popularity.

2011:

Bootstrap (an HTML, CSS, and JS framework for developing responsive, mobile-based web applications) is launched.

Laravel (a PHP web framework) is launched.

2012:

Webpack (a module bundler) is launched.

Grunt (a build/task manager written on top of NodeJS) is launched.

Composer (a tool for dependency management in PHP) is launched.

2013:
> React (a JavaScript library created by Facebook) is released.

2014:
> Vue.js (a progressive framework for building UI/UX interfaces) is launched.

2017:
> Yarn (a new JavaScript package manager built by Facebook, Google, Exponent, and Tilde) is released.

In today's software development world, gone are the days when a developer would be sitting with others in front of a computer screen simply churning out code in order to create a particular web application. Rather, the web apps of today take large project management teams, which are located worldwide and virtually.

Thus, the use of project management methodologies is now the norm, and it is important to look at the timeline of the evolution of this and how they have contributed to creating efficient and large-scale web applications.

The 1950s:
> This era saw the birth of structured programming. Block structures, subroutines, and FOR and WHILE loops are extensively used in creating source code.

The 1960s:
> This era saw the launch of the waterfall methodology. This is a sequential, noniterative process that has the following steps:
> - Requirement Analysis
> - Design
> - Implementation
> - Source Code Verification
> - Maintenance

The 1970s:
> This era saw the rise of iterative and incremental methodology. The purpose of this framework is to develop source code through repeated cycles. This is done in smaller chunks at a time in order to make sure that any development issues have been resolved in previous iterations.

The 1980s:
> During this time frame, three major software development methodologies were created, as follows:
> 1. Prototyping:
>   This involves creating various prototypes of software applications before they are launched into a production environment. The steps include the following:
>   - Identify the basic requirements
>   - Develop the initial prototype

- Review the prototype
- Revise and enhance the prototype

2. The Spiral Methodology:
   This is considered to be a much more risk-driven approach.

3. The V-Model:
   This considered to be an extension of the waterfall methodology and consists of the following components:
   - Concept of operations
   - Requirements and architecture
   - Detailed design
   - Integration, test, and verification
   - System verification and validation
   - Operation and maintenance

1990s:
   This era gave rise to the rapid application development methodology. As the name implies, the goal is to create source code in a quick fashion, with more emphasis being placed upon processes, adaptability, and changing requirements. It consists of the following components:
   - Requirements analysis and quick coding
   - Demonstration of the source code
   - Testing
   - Implementation

The 2000s:
   This is the birth of the various agile software development methodologies. The goal here is to implement adaptive planning, evolutionary development, early delivery, and continuous development. Ten different methodologies were launched, as follows:

1. The Unified Process:
   The characteristics here include:
   - Iterative and incremental
   - Architecture-centric
   - A risk-focused approach

2. The Dynamic Systems Development:
   The components here include:
   - Prototyping
   - Testing
   - Demonstrative workshops
   - Modeling
   - Configuration management

3. Scrum:
   This encourages very close collaboration among the software development team, as well as daily face-to-face interactions.

4. Extreme Programming:
   Short software development cycles and quick releases are the norm here, as well as many checkpoints in order to confirm the validity of the source code.
5. Crystal:
   This is designed to be a lightweight approach, with a specific set of policies, procedures, and processes in the source code development.
6. Feature-Driven Development:
   The goal here is to deliver source code modules in a repetitive and timely manner. It consists of the following components:
   • Develop the overall model
   • Build the feature list
   • Plan by the feature
   • Design by the feature
   • Build the feature
7. The Agile Unified Process:
   This methodology applies to the following:
   • Test-driven development (TDD)
   • Agile modeling (AM)
   • Agile change management (ACM)
   • Database refactoring
8. The Disciplined Agile Delivery:
   This is a process-driven framework in which a decision-making process is enabled around incremental and iterative solution delivery.
9. The Scaled Agile Framework (SAFe):
   This is a software development methodology that consists of integrated patterns meant for enterprise-scaled lean-agile–based source code development.
10. Large-Scale Scrum (LeSS):
    This is the scrum methodology, but applied to enterprise-scale web application development.

The Fundamentals of Network Security – The OSI Model

The OSI Model

Before we dive into the fundamentals of network security, it is first important to review one of the theoretical models that is used widely today by many businesses and corporations in order to establish their respective network infrastructures. This model is known as the Open Systems Interconnect model, or OSI for short.

The OSI model describes how a network protocol or firmly established infrastructure will communicate among one another. A perfect example of this is two major network segments connected together. For instance, this could be a LAN-to-LAN connection, a WAN-to-WAN connection, or even a LAN-to-WAN connection. These examples are merely a 1:1 mathematical relationship, but there are many instances in which several LANs and WANs are connected together. This is all done via the OSI model.

This model was established by the International Organization for Standards (ISO) back in the 1980s, thus establishing its strong credibility in the world of IT. The following matrix describes each component of the OSI model.

The Network Layer	The Description	The Supported Protocols
Application	This layer interfaces directly to the applications and performs common services for the application processes.	POP, SMTP, DNS, FTP, Telnet
Presentation	This relieves the application layer from having to deal with syntactical differences in the data representation within the various end-user systems	Telnet, Network Data Representation (NDR), and the Lightweight Presentation Protocol (LPP)
Session	This layer provides the mechanism for managing the dialogue between the end-user application processes.	NetBIOS
Transport	This provides end-to-end communications control.	TCP, UDP
Network	This provides the information and data to the network.	IP, ARP, ICMP
Data Link	This supports the logical organization of data bits that are transmitted on a particular medium. This layer is divided into different sublayers: the Media Access Control (MAC) layer and the Logical Link Control (LLC) layer.	SLIP, PPP
Physical	This supports the physical properties of the various communications media, as well as the electrical properties and the interpretation of the exchanged signals. These refer to the network interface card (NIC), Ethernet cabling, etc.	IEEE 1394, DSL, ISDN

What Is the Significance of the OSI Model to Network Security?

The OSI touches the security realm in three different areas, which are as follows:

1. The Data:
   After the data packets leave a network infrastructure, they are extremely vulnerable in terms of interception and even loss of integrity by a malicious third party, such as a cyberattacker.
2. The Network Connection Points:
   Anywhere that devices are connected together via a network medium (whether it is hard wired or wireless) is prone to a cyberattack. As a result, these weak spots must obviously be protected to the greatest extent possible, and this is where the role of endpoint security and threat hunting comes into play. This will be reviewed in much greater detail in Chapter 4 of this book.
3. The Individuals Involved:
   Individuals, especially those employed by a business or a corporation, can pose the greatest security threat. This can be through sheer ignorance of the security policies that have been set, having a malicious intent (in this instance, insider attacks are very common and very hard to detect), or even just by simple, nonintentional errors.

The Classification of Threats to the OSI Model

The specific threats encompass three broad categories, which are as follows:

1. Intrusion:
   This category includes the various forms of cyberattacks that are meant to breach the lines of defense and gain unauthorized access to a particular system.
2. Blocking:
   This category includes cyberattacks that are designed to prevent legitimate end-user access to a particular system. These kinds of cyberattacks are also known as DDoS. The purpose of this kind of cyberattack is not to actually cause any sort of damage to your network infrastructure per se, but the intent is to simply completely block legitimate end users from accessing the shared resources that are available on a server(s).
3. Malware:
   This is a general, all-purpose term for a piece of software that has any malicious intent built into it. For instance, this can include viruses, Trojan horses, and even spyware. This has been deemed to be the most common threat to any network infrastructure, largely because they have been designed to spread

themselves on their own, quickly and covertly. The following are the most common forms of malware:

— Viruses:

These are specifically defined as "… a program that can infect other programs by modifying them to include a possibly evolved copy of itself." The most common method by which viruses are spread is via email, when the end-user's address book has been hacked into by the cyberattacker.

— Trojan Horses:

As a brief background, this specific term is borrowed from an ancient tale. The city of Troy was under attack for a long time, but the intruders for some reason or another could not gain entrance through the main gates. Because of this, the attackers thus constructed a large wooden horse and left it one night in the city. The citizens of the city assumed that this was some sort of gift and rolled into the main square. But unbeknownst to these citizens, this horse actually contained a few of the intruders that were trying to gain access. When the citizens were not actually looking, these intruders then left the horse and then opened up the gates so that all of the intruders could enter the city of Troy. This is how the electronic version of the Trojan horse works. For example, the intended victim is offered an enticing gift that gets installed onto your computer or wireless device. But in the end, this is an actual piece of malicious software.

— Spyware:

This is yet another form of a Trojan horse, but is more devastating and covert. For example, probably the simplest of this is the cookie. This is a simple text file that your web browser creates and stores on your hard drive. These are designed so that you can access the same website more quickly, rather than having to type in the same URL or domain name over and over again. But in order for this to actually work, this text file must read by the website in question, which in turn means that this can be even be read by other websites, and because of that, your entire browsing history can thus be tracked, causing a grave network security risk.

— Key Loggers:

This is another form of malware, but it is a piece of malicious software that covertly records your keystrokes. It can even take secret screenshots of your computer or wireless device. The information and data that are recorded are subsequently sent back to the cyberattacker. It is important to note here that every single thing you type on your computer is recorded.

4. Intrusions:

These are cyberattacks that are actually trying to intrude into a system in your network infrastructure. It is important to note that it could be hacker breaking in from the external environment, or it very well could be an insider attack from within your business or corporation. These kinds of cyberattacks run the gamut from simply denying users access to a particular system (this is known as "blocking") or those kinds of hacks that are not too focused, such as that of viruses and worms, as previously reviewed. Those types of intrusion attacks that are much more targeted towards a specific system are typically referred to as "hacking." However, the cyberattacker has their own term for this, and it is called "cracking," which simply means invading a particular system without any sort of explicit level of permission. In most of these cases, the idea is to exploit some kind of software flaw or vulnerability in order to gain covert access. However, another form of intrusion that does not require that much technology is known as social engineering. In these instances, the cyberattacker gains preliminary information and data about the target organization. From this point, the goal is to use this knowledge in order to gain more information by tricking the employees. The bottom line is that social engineering is based upon how well the cyberattacker can manipulate people and actually has very little to do with possessing deep levels of technological skills. Another example of an intrusion attack is known as "war driving." This kind of scenario takes advantage of exploiting the weaknesses and vulnerabilities that are found in a wireless network. War driving is actually a subset of "war dialing." This is when a cyberattacker sets up a computer to call cell phone numbers in a sequential fashion until a computer actually picks up on the call in order to gain access to the wireless network. But war driving is used to detect any vulnerabilities in a wireless network itself. Wireless connections are not totally safe either, as they can extend well beyond 100 feet.

5. Distributed Denial of Service:

   As was reviewed earlier, the cyberattacker in this kind of scenario does not access a particular system, but simply blocks access to legitimate end users. Typically, servers are the primary target. This kind of attack can be specifically defined as follows: "It is characterized by an explicit attempt by a cyberattacker to prevent legitimate end users of a service from using that shared resource." One form of a DDoS attack is when the cyberattacker floods the targeted system with millions of false connection requests such that the servers' processing and computing power are brought down.

The Most Probable Attacks

Now that we have reviewed some of the major cyberattacks that can affect a network infrastructure and the associated web applications that it hosts, the question now arises is which ones are most likely to affect a business or corporation. According to a study conducted by McAfee, the virus is the most prevalent threat.

The primary reason for this is that many people simply do not update their antivirus software as it is needed or required. It is a known fact that if all of the computer systems and networks in the world adhered to a regular patch and software upgrade schedule, there would not be that many occurrences of virus attacks.

The next cyberattack that is likely to occur is that of blocking. The main reason for this is that they are much easier to launch than intrusion-based cyberattacks.

But whatever threat vector is used, the fact remains that cyberattacks are largely prevalent in today's society and will continue to be so. For instance, 32% of organizations in corporate America have been affected by a cyberattack, with losses amounting to well over $5 million.

Assessing a Threat to a Web Application

When conducting this kind of study, the chief information officer (CIO) or chief information security officer (CISO) must consider a number of factors. The first one is the level of attractiveness to a cyberattacker. For example, this could be based upon the monetary value of a network infrastructure or because it is high profile in nature. Cyberattackers currently seem to be the most attracted to government and computer security types of web applications because they are simply high profile in nature. Also, those web applications that are hosted by universities and colleges are a much-favored target.

The second risk factor that must be taken into consideration is the kind of confidential information and data that reside in the database of a web application. Examples of this include Social Security numbers, credit card and banking numbers, and medical records/data.

The third risk factor that must be evaluated is the network traffic that is coming into the web application. Obviously, the more people that have remote access to the back end (in particular, the database), the more security dangers will naturally exist.

Once all of these risk factors have been evaluated and compiled, the following numerical scale can then be used in order to further quantify them:

- The level of attractiveness: It receives a ranking of 1 if the system is virtually unknown to a cyberattacker but receives a ranking of 10 if is completely known to a cyberattacker, thus making it a prime target.
- The level of confidential information and data: It receives a ranking of 1 if the system has no confidential information and data that reside within it, but receives a ranking of 10 if a lot of information and data reside on it, thus making it a prime target.
- The network traffic: A web application receives a ranking of 10 if it is extensively layered. It has a proactive security system outfitted with firewalls, ports are blocked, antivirus software is installed, it is protected by an intrusion detection system (IDS), the appropriate security policies are put into place, etc. If none of these are present, then the web application receives a ranking of 1.

In compiling the total risk factor score, the first two categories are added together, and the third category is subtracted from the summation of the first two. Thus, the risk factor scores will range from −8 (which represents a very low risk and high security type of web application) to 19 (which represents a very high risk and low security type of web application). In other words, the lower the number, the less vulnerable the web application is to a cyberattack, but the higher the number, the greater the risk.

Network Security Terminology

In the world of network security, and even that of cybersecurity, there are a lot of terms, acronyms, and the proverbial "techno-jargon." Unfortunately, this list never stops; it keeps growing and growing as the number of cyberattacks keep growing and become much more sophisticated. But for the purposes of this chapter, we are not going to review all of these definitions and terms; instead, we are only going to present those that have the most relevance to the content in this book.

These terms are as follows:

1. The Firewall:
   In general terms, a firewall can be defined as a "… barrier between a network and the outside world." It is important to note that a firewall can be a stand-alone server (for example, a router or even just a software application). But whatever form that it does take, the primary objective of a firewall still remains the same: to filter out network traffic that is entering and exiting an entire IT infrastructure. Very often a firewall will be situated just behind what is known as a "proxy server." This masks all of the IP addresses that are currently being used in a network infrastructure and presents just a single IP address to the outside world. Firewalls can also be used in conjunction with IDSs in order to spot malicious and/or anomalous activity.
2. Access Control:
   This can be specifically defined as "… the aggregate of all measures that are taken to limit access to resources." Examples of this typically include logon procedures that are set forth in the security policies of the business or corporation, encryption (which will be covered in more detail in Chapter 2), or any other defined method that is designed to prevent unauthorized access to a shared, network-based resource. A subset of access control is "access control," and this is defined as "… the process of determining whether the credentials given by a user are authorized to access the network resource in question."
3. Nonrepudiation:
   This can be defined as a method or a technique "… that is used to ensure that someone performing an action on a computer, wireless device, or any other

IT asset from within a network infrastructure cannot falsely deny that he or she actually performed that action." In other words, these are detailed records of when an end user took a particular action at a specific point in time. One of the best ways to do this is through a technique known as auditing. This is the actual process of the IT security staff or even the network administrator reviewing logs, records, and other security-related procedures.

4. Least Privileges:
   When developing web-based applications that will be hosted on a sever, this is one of the most important concepts to deploy, especially when it comes to software developers and other employees in your organization. This is when you only assign the bare minimum of privileges, rights, and permissions that are required for an employee to conduct their daily tasks.

The Types of Network Security Topologies Best Suited for Web Applications

Obviously many security-related models are available that can be used to protect any type of web application that is hosted on a server, but the following are the most commonly used. Deciding which one to adopt and implement is largely dependent upon the security requirements of your organization.

The models are as follows:

1. The Perimeter Security Model:
   This kind of model is only used when the lines of defense that define the external environment and the internal environment of a business or corporation need to be clearly defined and thus fortified. This includes the use of any type of security tool (primarily firewalls and routers) that makes access to a particular network infrastructure almost impossible.
2. The Layered Security Model:
   This kind of model is used for both the perimeter of the business or corporation and its internal network infrastructure in which the web applications reside. This means providing strong levels of protection for all of the servers, workstations, firewalls, routers, bridges, and hubs and that they are deemed to be 100% secure. Probably the best way to accomplish this task is to divide your entire network infrastructure into different trunks, or segments. That way, if a security breach were to occur, it will not affect the entire network infrastructure.
3. The Hybrid Security Model:
   This model is a combination both the perimeter security–based and layered security–based models, and as a result, this offers the maximum levels of protection to a web application that resides within a network infrastructure.

The Types of Attack That Can Take Place against Web Applications

In this section of this chapter, we will examine in much more detail the specific types of cyberattacks that can affect a particular web application. We touched on them earlier in this chapter, but now we get into much more technical detail in how they are launched and executed.

1. The DDoS Attack:

    The goal here is to deprive legitimate end users of a target server on which the web applications reside. This type of attack really is not designed to infiltrate a server per se, or even capture confidential information and data. Rather, the primary goal of this kind of cyberattack is to prevent end users from gaining access to shared resources. This kind of cyberattack is one of the most common ones to occur on an almost daily basis. The concept behind the DDoS attack is based upon the fact that any device, whether it is a computer, server, wireless device, etc., has its own set of operational limits in terms of workload capacity. This can be defined in a variety of ways, which include the following variables:

    - The number of simultaneous end users that can be served at the same time
    - The file size of the shared resources
    - The speed of the network data transmission (whether it is hard wired or wireless)
    - The amount of information and data that are stored which need to be accessed

    Probably one of the best ways to understand how a DDoS attack actually works is to simulate this on an actual computer. In order to do this, you will need to have access to a web server service. You can use either the Microsoft Internet Information Server or the Apache-based HTTP Server. Make sure that you use an older computer or server in order to download either of these two web server services in order to fully grasp how a DDoS really works. The premise behind this is that the older the machine is, the quicker it will be to respond to a simulated DDoS attack because of its slower processing and computational powers.

    For purposes of this chapter, we will examine a simulated DDoS attack using the Apache HTTP Server.

    If you are using a Windows operating system:
    - Download Apache for Windows at www.apache.org.
    - Once it is downloaded, look for the following directory structure:
      C:\Program Files\Apache Group\Apache2\conf
      This will contain the httpd.conf files that you need.

- Set the server to ServerName = localhost.
- Save the file.
- Launch the command line (from the MS DOS prompt) and type in https start.

If you are using a Linux operating system:
- Download Apache for Linux at www.apache.org.
- Once it is downloaded, look for the following directory structure:

```
/etc/httpd/conf
```

This will contain the httpd.conf files that you need.
- Set the server to ServerName = localhost.
- Save the file.
- From a shell, type in the following command:

```
/etc/init.d/httpd start
```

This will initiate the Apache Web Service.
- Open up a web browser and go the following:
  http://localhost/
- In order to make the Apache HTTP Server go live, change the following settings:
  - Change "servername" to your own domain or IP address.
  - Change "listen" to reflect the IP address and the port number that you want to use.
  - Check the "documentroot" directory to confirm that this is where you want your web pages to be served from. It is important to note that the default setting should be:

  ```
  /var/www/html
  ```

  - From a shell, type in the following command:

  ```
  /etc/init.d/httpd start
  ```

It is also important to note at this point that in order to change any configuration settings to the Apache HTTP Server, you will first need to stop the server, and this can be done by entering in the following command:

```
/etc/init.d/http stop
```

Now, you are ready to launch your simulated DDoS attack. To do this, you will execute the "ping" command. Follow these steps:
- Type in ping/h.

This particular command will show all of the options that are available for the ping command, which are as follows:

- - w: This option will determine how many milliseconds it will actually take for the Ping utility to wait for a response from your server. For purposes of this demonstration, set this option to -0, so that the Ping utility will not have to wait at all.
- - t: This instructs the Ping utility to keep sending data packets until it is explicitly told to stop. With the -1 you can change the size of the data packets that are sent. It is important to keep in mind that a TCP-based data packet must be a finite size.

— At the shell in the Linux operating system, type in the following:

- ping <IP Address of target server goes here> -1 6500 -w -t.

What is happening now is that your Apache HTTP Server is being flooded with an excessive number of ping commands, and eventually the processing power will reach its limits, and the Apache Server should eventually crash and not respond to any more requests. Generally speaking, the methods that are used by a cyberattacker to launch a real-world DDoS attack are far more sophisticated and covert. For example, he or she could very easy easily craft a virus whose only purpose is to initiate a large-scale Ping attack against a selected server or group of servers. This virus in turn could spread itself to other servers on a global basis, causing a grave, cascading effect. As mentioned previously, DDoS attacks are one of the most popular threat vectors for the cyberattacker, for two primary reasons:

— It is easy to do.
— The cyberattacker can launch a DDoS attack from another computer or server, thus masking their identity. If they launched it from their own infrastructure, the data packets could be traced back to it.

2. The SYN Flood:

The SYN flood is a more sophisticated type of DDoS attack. In order to launch this particular threat vector, the cyberattacker must have a deep knowledge of how network connections are established and maintained to a server that hosts a web application. When a session is initiated between the client and the server using the TCP/IP protocol, a small buffer in memory is created in order to create what is known as a "handshaking" exchange of messages, which actually establishes the network session.

This type of session establishing includes what is known as a SYN field, which specifically identifies the sequences in the message exchange. The goal of the SYN flood is to actually subvert this entire process. In other words, the cyberattacker sends a number of connection requests in a rapid-fire fashion and then subsequently never follows up with the reply that is sent back by that server. As a result, this has the effect of leaving the network connection on the server half-open, and the buffer memory that is allocated for these connections is thus reserved and not available to other web applications that are hosted on that server.

Although the data packets that are in the memory buffer are discarded after about three minutes without a reply from the sender (in this case, the cyberattacker), the effect of sending hundreds or even thousands of requests all at once makes it difficult for the legitimate requests for a network session to get fully established.

One of the primary reasons why SYN flooding is so popular is that any server which engages in a TCP/IP-based network connection is vulnerable to it – and pretty much all of the servers use the TCP/IP protocol in order to establish a network connection between the end user and the web application. But there are numerous ways in which to defend against a SYN Flood attack, and these are as follows:

— Using Micro Blocks:

This method changes the way in which the server allocates the memory space for any connection request that it might receive. For example, instead of allocating a complete connection, the server can be altered so that it only allocates what is known as a "micro-record." Newer methods of micro blocks can allocate as little as 16 bytes for the incoming SYN object.

— Using Bandwidth Throttling:

This is when the firewall, router, or IDS detects any sort of excessive network-based traffic coming from one or more IP addresses. If this is detected, the bandwidth to the server is drastically restricted and scaled back.

— Using SYN Cookies:

With this method, the server does not immediately create a buffer space in its memory in order to initiate the handshaking process. Instead, it first sends a SYNACK message. This is an acknowledgement signal that actually initiates the handshaking process. The SYNACK consists of a very carefully crafted cookie, which is generated as a hash that contains the port number, the IP address, and any other information and data coming in from the computer of the end user that is requesting a network connection. When the computer of the end user responds with an ACK (or acknowledgement message), the information and data generated by that cookie will be verified by the server to which the network connection will be established. However, using this kind of defense mechanism is intense in terms of processing power, and because of that, this method is not as commonly used. In other words, this particular defense mechanism illustrates the fact that there is a trade-off between performance and security.

— Using RST Cookies:

With this method, the server intentionally sends a wrong SYNACK message back to the computer of the end user. In response to this, the client computer will then generate an RST (or Reset) data packet that notifies the server that there is something wrong in establishing a network connection. Because of this, the server now understands that this is actually a legitimate request that is coming from the computer of the end user and will thus subsequently establish the network connection that is requested. But a firewall or a router could very well block the return SYNACK data packet.

– Using Stack Tweaking:

This method involves altering the TCP stack on the server so that it will take less time to time out in the instance that a SYN connection still remains incomplete. But when compared to the other defensive methods just reviewed, this is the most complex one.

Probably the most efficient way in which to defend against a DDoS attack is to use a combination of these defense mechanisms. For example, using both SYN cookies and RST cookies in conjunction with stack tweaking is deemed to be the best defensive mechanism thus far.

3. The Smurf Attack:

This is yet another form of a DDoS attack. In this kind of cyberattack, an Internet Control Message Protocol (ICMP)–based data packet is transmitted to the broadcast address of any network infrastructure. But in return, its specific address has been altered in such a way that it matches up to one of the IP addresses on the network. In return, all of the computers, workstations, and wireless devices will then respond back by pinging this server.

It should be noted that the ICMP-based data packets use ICMP to transmit error messages over the Internet. But because the addresses on these kinds of data packets are sent to a broadcast address, that address responds back by echoing that data packet to all of the hosts that reside on that network infrastructure, which in turn will send out a spoofed source address.

By constantly sending out all of these data packets, this in itself will cause the network infrastructure to perform a DDoS attack on one of its own servers. This is actually a rather sophisticated attack, but the main difficulty is in launching the data packets onto a target network infrastructure. But this can be accomplished by making use of a virus or a Trojan horse to execute the start of the flow of the data packets.

In a smurf attack, the network infrastructure performs a DDoS attack on itself. But there are two ways in which in which you can protect your network infrastructure from a smurf attack, which are as follows:

– You can configure all of your routers in such a way that they do not forward any sort of broadcast-based data packets. If they are transmitted, the smurf attack is then very often contained to a subnetwork (which is just a trunk of the entire network infrastructure).

– You can simply protect your network infrastructure by guarding against Trojan horses. But this is actually easier said than done, because your employees have to abide by your security policies, which must clearly state the dangers of downloading questionable attachments or even clicking on malicious links.

- You should also make use of a proxy server. In these instances, they can mask the internal IP addresses of the computers, servers, and wireless devices that reside within your network infrastructure.

4. The Ping of Death:

This is probably one of the most basic forms of a DDoS attack. In these instances, the TCP-based data packets are of a limited size, and even sending just one that is too large can bring an entire server down. Thus, the primary goal of the Ping of Death attacks is to compromise those servers that simply cannot process or handle data packets that are large in size. Thus, this kind of cyberattack latches itself onto those vulnerabilities in the way that an operating system or even a software application responds to abnormally sized data packets.

5. The UDP Flood:

User Datagram Protocol (UDP) is a type of network-based protocol that is connectionless. In other words, it does not require any form of connection in which to transfer the data packets. The TCP data packets are connected when the computer of the end user acknowledges its receipt. There is no confirmation involved here, and this allows for the data packets to be transmitted much faster, thus making it a lot easier to perform a DDoS attack.

6. The ICMP Flood:

This is just another variant of the flood attack described previously, but the ICMP-based data packets also make use of the tracert structure (in Windows operating systems, this is known as "tracert" and in Linux operating systems, this is known as "traceroute").

7. DCHP Starvation:

If enough ping requests are sent over to the network infrastructure, the cyberattacker can completely exhaust all of the IP address spaces that are allocated to the DHCP servers for an indefinite period of time.

8. The HTTP Post DoS:

In this kind of cyberattack, a legitimate post message is transmitted, but it contains a "content length." This merely indicates the size of the messages in the data packets that are to follow. Once all of this has been determined, the cyberattacker then transmits this actual message at a very, very slow rate. Because of this, the web server is then literally "hung up" awaiting for that message to be completed.

9. The PDoS:

This is an acronym that stands for "permanent denial of service." The goal here is to permanently damage a server so that it has to be completely replaced by launching a DDoS attack against the firmware of the server. This kind of attack is also known as "phlashing."

10. The Distributed Reflection Denial of Service:
    With this kind of cyberattack, the goal is to trick the routers into launching a DDoS attack against a specific server. It is important to note that many routers communicate among one another on port 179. The cyberattacker thus exploits any vulnerabilities or weaknesses that are found in those network connections that are going to port 179. What is so dangerous about this kind of cyberattack is that the cyberattacker sends a constant stream of data packets to the routers in question by requesting a network connection. In turn, the data packets that get transmitted are altered in such a way that they appear to originate from the target server's IP address. The routers then respond by initiating network connections to that target server. As a result, a constant flood of network connections from multiple routers hit the same target server, making it totally unreachable by the computers, workstations, and wireless devices of the end user.

How to Protect Web Applications from DDoS Attacks

Unfortunately in the real world, there is no 100% guaranteed way to protect your business or corporation from a DDoS attack. But the key is to have a proactive mind-set and to make sure that your security tools (such as your routers, network intrusion devices, firewalls, etc.) are strategically placed to give you maximum protection. Remember, technology alone cannot do it. It takes a combination of all of these approaches.

One of the first things you should consider is researching how DDoS attacks are launched in the first place. More than likely, as reviewed in length, the two most widely used threat vehicles are those of using ICMP data packets to send false messages and using the Ping and traceroute functionalities. One of the best ways to defend against this is to fine-tune the configuration of your firewall to simply refuse ICMP data packets from the external environment coming into your network infrastructure. A much more radical step would be to simply disallow all data packets from coming in, but this should only be done in extreme cases.

If your network infrastructure is large enough to have internal routers from within it, you can also configure them so that they do not allow any kind of data packets to enter in. In a way, the router acts as a secondary step in a two-factor authentication (2FA) approach. For example, the firewall would be the first line of defense, and the router would be the second line of defense. That way, if a malicious data packet did make it past the firewall, it will not be allowed to go any further by the router.

Because all TCP-based data packets have a source IP address, ascertaining where they originated from (such as whether they came from inside or outside your network infrastructure) is not a difficult task to accomplish. Another option in this regard is to totally disable all forms of directed IP broadcasts across all of the internal routers. But once again, this is an extreme measure and should only be used as a last resort.

Other steps you can take to protect your organization from a DDoS attack are:

- Always keep the antimalware and antispyware scanning software on your servers at all times.
- Keep the operating systems of all computers, workstations, and wireless devices updated.
- Strictly enforce your security policy by not allowing your employees to download anything unless they have the permission of the IT security staff.

Another comprehensive way to protect your business or corporation is to conduct a penetration test. This will reveal in much more detail all of the known and unknown security vulnerabilities that exist in your lines of defense. In fact, this topic is exclusively covered in Chapter 3 of this book.

The rest of the section will examine in further detail how you can protect your business or corporation from specific types of DDoS attacks.

Defending against Buffer Overflow Attacks

Another common way to attack your network infrastructure is called a "buffer overflow." Simply put, this kind of attack is designed to put more data into a buffer memory – much more than it can hold. For example, when the end user communicates with the web application and vice versa, any information and/or data that is transmitted is stored temporarily in a space called the "buffer." Normally, the buffer will truncate or reject any data packets that exceed a pre-established threshold.

In these instances, the cyberattacker will more than likely flood the buffer memory onto the target sever. This will then have the effect of overwriting the other pieces of information and data that are currently in the memory buffer, thus causing the server to crash.

Probably the best way to defend against these types of attacks is to have the source code that is compiled for the web application to be 100% secure. Of course, in the real world, this is not technically possible, so in the end, the best defense is to make sure that you apply the latest software patches and upgrades that come out and deploy them on a timely basis.

Defending against IP Spoofing Attacks

This is a technique that used by the cyberattacker in order to gain unauthorized access to computers, workstations, and other wireless devices that reside within a network infrastructure. Although this is the primary goal for launching an IP spoofing attack, it can also be used to mask the actual origins of a DDoS attack. With this sort of attack, the cyberattacker sends various messages to the systems within the network infrastructure, indicating that the message is coming from a totally different IP address than where it is originating from.

If the primary intent of the cyberattacker is to gain unauthorized access to the shared network resources, it is quite likely that the spoofed IP address will be that of a system which is considered to be a trusted host. In order to successfully launch such a cyberattack, the cyberattacker must first locate and determine the IP address of a server that is deemed to be that of a trusted host.

Once this has been accomplished, the cyberattacker can then modify the headers of the data packets during their transmission across the medium from the web application to the end user's computer, and vice versa. This will ultimately appear as if these data packets are coming from the trusted host.

Quite surprisingly, IP spoofing was known by computer scientists in the academic sector, at least on a theoretical level, before it was even launched as a "true" cyberattack. This goes as far back as the early 1980s. It continued to remain on a theoretical level until a computer scientist, Robert Morris, discovered a security flaw in the TCP-based protocol. This was technically known as "sequence prediction," and more details of this breakthrough can be found in the scientific paper he wrote entitled "Security Problems in the TCP/IP Protocol Suite."

It should be noted that IP spoofing attacks are becoming much less frequent, primarily because the threat vehicles that are used to launch them are becoming much more secure. However, any cyberattacker can still launch this type of attack on a whim. In order to prevent against an IP spoofing attack, the following is recommended:

■ Do not in any way reveal the internal IP addresses of either your IT or network infrastructures.
■ You must always monitor for incoming data packets that are malicious or are indicative of an IP spoofing attack. Thus, it is always important to use the necessary software applications in these situations. They monitor the influx of data packets that originate from the external environment, which contain both the source and destination addresses of your IT and network infrastructures. As a result, any data packet that "claims" to be coming from your internal infrastructure will be immediately tagged when the evidence clearly shows that they are coming from the external environment.

One of the biggest dangers of IP spoofing is that not all firewalls examine for data packets that look like they are coming from an internal IP address. Thus, the routing of data packets through various filtering routers is quite possible if they are not specifically configured to filter for incoming data packets when the source address resides clearly in the local domain.

Some typical examples of those router configurations that are vulnerable to an IP spoofing attack include the following:

■ Routers that interface to an external network which supports multiple types of internal interfaces

- Proxy firewalls in which the proxy applications make use of the source IP address for authentication purposes
- Those routers that have two interfaces which allow for the subnetting of an internal-based network
- Those types of routers that do not filter for data packets in which their source address clearly resides in the local domain.

Probably one of the best ways to protect against an IP spoofing attack is to deploy and implement what is known as a filtering router. These types of routers filter for incoming data packets by simply not allowing a data packet to enter into the network infrastructure if it actually contains a source address that is different from your internal network.

On top of this, you should also filter for those outgoing data packets which have a source IP address that is different from the pool of IP addresses that are from the internal network infrastructure as well. The result of this is that it will prevent an IP spoofing attack from originating within your network infrastructure. Keep in mind also that you can even use two or more routers in order to block the outgoing interface connected to the original router.

Defending against Session Hijacking

Another major threat that is posed to web applications is session hijacking. This is a specific process in which the cyberattacker can take over a TCP-based session between two servers. Since most authentication takes place only at the start of a network communications session, the cyberattacker can thus break easily into this line of communication (of course, unless a virtual private network, or VPN, is being used) and take total command of it. A typical example of this is the remote employee at a business or corporation. Whenever he or she remotely logs in, the cyberattacker can break through any vulnerabilities or weaknesses that are present, and from there, gain control of the server upon which the web application resides.

One of the most widely used vehicles to launch session hijacking is to make use of source-routed IP data packets. For example, if a cyberattacker is on point X in a network communications stream, he or she can gain access to points B and C by allowing these IP-based data packets to filter through the cyberattacker's own server.

The most common form of session hijacking is what is known as a "man in the middle attack." In these instances, the cyberattacker makes use of a data packet sniffing program in order to listen in on the network communications line between the end user's computer and the server that hosts the web application. From this point, the cyberattacker can then covertly gather any kind of information and data that they want.

A critical component of a man in the middle attack is to actually launch the DDoS attack against one endpoint so it will stop responding to any type of requests that come to it. As a result of this, the cyberattacker can then put his or her own server in front of that unresponsive endpoint. In other words, the primary goal of this cyberattack is to exploit any vulnerabilities or weaknesses that are detected in the network lines of communication and gain access to the target server upon which the web application resides.

In the end, the only true way to prevent this kind of cyberattack is to utilize some sort of encrypted transmission, such as a VPN. It is also important to keep in mind that a cyberattacker can also make use of what is known as a data sniffer. This is a software-based tool that can very easily intercept data packets going across a wireless network and copies the data packets that are sent and received.

Defending Virus and Trojan Horse Attacks

Viruses

In technical terms, a virus is merely a malicious program that replicates itself and has rapid-fire spread. One of the primary goals of a virus is to greatly reduce both the functionality and the overall responsiveness of a network infrastructure. This is simply done by exceeding the traffic load that a network infrastructure has been designed to carry.

How a Virus Spreads Itself

A virus can be spread to a web application in two fashions:

■ Scanning a server for connections to a specific part of the network infrastructure (this is also known as a "subnet") and from that point, copying itself to other servers on other, different network segments.
■ Hijacking the email address book of the end user that is accessing the web application and replicating and sending itself to all of the contacts in that particular address book. In this regard, a virus can delete files, change server settings, or even cause greater harm.

The Different Types of Viruses

As we all know, in the world of cybersecurity, many different kinds of viruses exist. In this section, we outline some of the major classifications of viruses and how they can affect a web application:

1. The Macro Virus:
   These kinds of viruses affect the macros found in Office-based documents. These are essentially mini programs that are often found in Microsoft Office

products, most notably that of Word and Excel. Although these macros have been designed to help automate routine processes on a very basic level, they can also be crafted to make them into viruses. In both Microsoft Word and Excel, a scripting language known as Visual Basic is used to develop these macros, whether it is for malicious purposes or not.

2. The Boot Sector:

As its name implies, this kind of virus does not actually affect the operating system (OS) of the server upon which the web application resides, but rather, it attacks the boot sector of the hard drive in the server. As a result, this makes them much harder to detect and remove with the traditional forms of antivirus software packages. Because these kinds of viruses can be launched outside of the operating system, the boot sector virus can be used as a covert and stealthy form of cyberattack. This has the potential to be a very nasty kind of virus, as it not only can affect the boot sector but can also delete mission-critical files that are needed to run the server upon which the web application resides.

3. The Stealth Virus:

This is deemed to be one of the largest groups of viruses present in the cyber-threat landscape of today. This category can be classified as a general one, in that the main intention of it is to avoid detection (thus its name, "stealth"). Typical examples of this kind of virus include the following:

- The polymorphic virus:

This virus changes its form and structure routinely in order to avoid detection by antivirus software applications. A much more advanced form of this is known as the metamorphic virus. This kind of virus can totally change its attack pattern in order to avoid detection.

- The sparse infector:

This kind of virus avoids detection in the sense that it delivers its malicious payload only on a very random basis, which makes it difficult to predict even for the most seasoned and experienced penetration testing and threat hunting teams. With this type of virus, the "symptoms" of it appear in an on and off cycle. For example, it may not be launched until the tenth or even the thirtieth time until the server that hosts the web application reboots itself. Or the opposite can happen. For example, it may demonstrate a huge burst of activity and then lie dormant for quite some time. The bottom line with this virus is that its primary goal is to avoid detection by keeping up with random launches that are very difficult to predict or even guess. Another example of this kind of virus is known as the fragmented payload. This one is split into various sorts of modules, with the main one being the loader module. The objective of this is to download all of the other fragments of the virus. When this has been accomplished, all of the modules will then be reassembled by the loader and the malicious payload will be launched.

– Ransomware:

At the present time, this is probably one of the most prevalent forms of viruses out there. The ultimate goal of this is to lock up the screen of the server upon which the web application resides, as well as the source code and other related files that are associated with it. In order to unlock the server and the files, the business or corporation must pay a ransom, usually in some sort of virtual currency, such as that of Bitcoin. But even when this is paid, there is no guarantee that the cyberattacker will send the decryption algorithms in order to unlock the server and the associated files. Probably the most famous and deadliest form of ransomware was known as WannaCry, and it attacked the healthcare systems in both the United Kingdom and Scotland. Actually, ransomware has been around for a long time, going as far back as even 1989, with the PC Cyborg Trojan. It is important to keep in mind that ransomware first starts out as a worm and then transforms itself into malware.

– The Trojan horse:

So far, the Trojan horse has been one of the prime examples that we have used in this chapter. Just to review, it may look benign to the end user, but it has a dangerous and malicious payload right behind it. The Trojan horse can be very tricky to detect at first, because it is usually first downloaded as an application (such as a game, or even a utility-based program). But once its payload is executed, any of the following repercussions could happen:

- It can download harmful software from any website that you may visit.
- It can install a keylogger or any other form of spyware onto the server.
- It can delete mission-critical files.
- It can open up a backdoor in the source code of the web application for the cyberattacker to enter into.

Defending Web Applications at a Deeper Level

Throughout this entire chapter, we have covered how to protect a web application from the standpoint of network security. In this section, we devote exclusive coverage to it, first starting with the firewall.

The Firewall

For the purposes of this book, a firewall can be defined specifically as follows: "A barrier between a server and an internal network from the outside world and/or the Internet." On a more technical level, a firewall is also referred to as a separation from the behind the demilitarized zone (DMZ) and the part of it that is made available to the public (remember, *the entire Internet* is not made available to the public – a lot of this consists of the Dark Web, which will be covered in a later chapter of this book).

A typical firewall can be configured as follows in order to protect the server upon which the web application resides:

- Packet filtering
- Stateful packet filtering
- User authentication
- Client application authentication

At the bare minimum level, a firewall should be able to filter the incoming data packets based on key variables such as the actual size of the data packet, the source IP address, any associated network protocols, and the destination port number. The most common types of firewalls are examined in the next subsections of this chapter.

Types of Firewalls

The following types of firewalls are used most often when it comes to securing web applications:

- Packet filtering firewalls
- Application gateway firewalls
- Circuit-level gateway firewalls
- Stateful inspection firewalls
- Hybrid firewalls

1. The Packet Filtering Firewall:
   This is type of firewall is deemed to be the most basic. With its specific set of configurations, each incoming data packet is carefully scrutinized. Only those data packets that match certain thresholds are allowed into the network infrastructure. This kind of firewall is also known as a screening firewall. They typically filter for data packet size, the network protocol that is being used, the source IP address, and a whole host of other variables.
   This kind of firewall works by examining the following:
   - The source IP address of the data packet
   - The destination IP address of the data packet
   - The source port
   - The destination port
   - The type of network protocol that is being used

Although it can be powerful to use when securing the server upon which the web application is hosted, there are a few disadvantages to it, which include the following:

- Because no history is kept of other data packets that have been allowed to enter into the network infrastructure, there is no baseline profile in which to make a comparison with. Thus, they are prone to either a Ping flood or a SYN flood type of cyberattack.
- There is no user authentication, so they are quite easily accessible.
- It only examines the data packet header; it does not examine what the data packet actually consists of.
- It cannot detect any unusual behavior in the flow of network traffic.

2. The Stateful Inspection Firewall:

This kind of firewall examines data packets that are not only in the current stream of network communications and also maintains a history of the data packets that have been allowed to enter the network infrastructure previously. This simply means that it is aware of the technical context in which previous data packets were sent. Thus, this makes them far less vulnerable to Ping or SYN flood attacks, unlike the packet filtering firewall.

It also has the following advantages:

- It can ascertain if a data packet is actually a subset of a much larger stream of data packets that exhibit abnormal or malicious types of behavior.
- It can determine if a particular data packet possesses a source IP address that appears to come from within the confines of the network infrastructure. If this is the case, then more than likely an IP spoofing attack is in progress.
- It can also examine the actual contents of a data packet and determine if it consists of any sort of malicious payload.
- It can examine the state of the data packet as it relates to the entire IP-based conversation between the web application and the computer, workstation, or wireless device of the end user that is accessing it.

3. The Application Gateway Firewall:

This is actually a software application that runs on a firewall. It can work with other different kinds of firewalls from within the network infrastructure in order to ascertain if a certain group of data packets should be allowed to enter a network infrastructure or not. In technical terms, this is also known as "negotiation" because a process of authentication and verification is utilized.

This software application will also carefully examine the flow of data packets from the web application as well as the server in which a connection is trying to be established. Thus, it will fully ascertain if the end user's computer, workstation, or wireless device is allowed to penetrate into the network infrastructure. The software application that runs on this kind of firewall is also known as a gateway or a proxy server.

Thus in the end, two types of connections are being made:
- The connection between the device of the end user and the proxy server
- The connection between the proxy server and the server that hosts the web application

Because of this two-way network transmission, all components that reside in the network infrastructure are made invisible to the outside world. Despite this advantage, this type of firewall demonstrates the following disadvantages:
- A lot of system resources (such as more memory and CPU processing time) are required in order to establish and maintain the two-way network flow of communications.
- It is prone to the various types of flooding attacks that have been covered so far in this chapter, for two primary reasons:
  - The additional time that is required for the software application to negotiate authenticating a request
  - Once the connection has been established from the proxy server to the web application server, it can be prone to a huge flooding attack

4. The Circuit-Level Gateway Firewall:

This kind of firewall is very similar to the application gateway firewall, but it is deemed to be far more secure. As a result, it is used in those areas of the network infrastructure that are deemed to be the most critical in nature. It also makes use of high levels of user authentication. With this system in place, and once the network connection has been established between the web application server and the end user's device, this firewall merely passes the bytes that are contained in the data packet between the two. Also, a "virtual" connection exists between the web application server and the end user. Any requests to the web application are transmitted through this particular circuit, and thus makes it secure in a manner very similar to that of a VPN. While this kind of firewall is the most robust in terms of security when compared to the others reviewed in this subsection, it may not be appropriate for web applications.

5. The Hybrid Firewall:

As its name implies, this kind of firewall utilizes a mix of approaches, as opposed to using just one type of approach. In fact, a mixed approach offers far more levels of security to a web application server. In this regard, the best mixture to use is that of circuit-level gateway firewall and a stateful packet filtering firewall.

Blacklisting and Whitelisting

All of the firewalls detailed in this subsection make use of what is known as blacklisting and whitelisting. Blacklisting is a security approach that makes the web application server accessible to virtually anybody in the business or corporation.

Of course, as one can see, this poses many security concerns, and thus is not utilized often, only when extreme circumstances dictate its use.

With whitelisting, the web application server is made available to only certain employees within the organization, and this is most likely just the IT staff and related security personnel.

How to Properly Implement a Firewall to Safeguard the Web Application

Now that we have examined the types of firewalls that can be used to protect a web application server, the next step is to make sure that it is properly implemented. If this not configured and deployed properly, then even using the best firewall available will not provide adequate layers of security. In this section, an overview is provided on how to do this properly by examining the four types of typical configurations that are used, which include the following:

- The network host–based configuration
- The dual-homed host configuration
- The router-based configuration
- The screened host configuration

1. The Network Host–Based Configuration:
   In this instance, the firewall is actually a software-based solution that is already installed onto a web application server that already has an operating system (such as Windows or Linux) running. Although this is a viable option to use, it is highly dependent upon how efficient the operating system is from the standpoint of security (for example, does it have all of the needed software upgrades and patches and even firmware installed onto it?).
   This is also referred to as operating system hardening, and it must reflect that the following safeguards have been deployed into it as well:
   - The uninstallation of unneeded software applications or utilities
   - The closure of unused ports
   - The turning off of all unused or unneeded network-based services
   The biggest advantage of using this kind of firewall configuration is that it is very cost-effective. For example, rather deploying a dedicated firewall to protect the web application server, it is far cheaper to just install a firewall software application onto it.
2. The Dual-Homed Host Configuration:
   This is a system in which the web application server is actually running at least two (or even more) network-based interfaces. In this case, the server itself acts as a router between the network infrastructure and the various interfaces that it is attached to. To make this an effective option, the "automatic routing"

functionality is completely disabled in the web application server, and this means that IP-based data packets coming in from the external environment are not immediately allowed to enter into the network infrastructure until they are inspected first. In fact, the IT security administrator can even select what kinds and types of data packets can be routed and the most optimal path in which they can be traversed from within the network infrastructure (this is assuming that they have passed the inspection, as just described). Also, any systems can communicate with the dual-homed host, but they cannot communicate directly with each other. But once again, this type of configuration is heavily dependent on how well hardened the operating system of the web application truly is.

3. The Router-Based Configuration:

As its name implies, this also a software application that resides upon a router. In those types of organizations where there are multiple layers of protection, this is often the first layer of defense that is utilized to protect the web server application. The most common type of software application that is used on a router is a packet filtering firewall. One of the best ways in which to protect the web application in these instances is to deploy them in between other network segments (which are known technically as subnets). In a way, this provides for a multilevel-layer security approach in the sense that if one of the software applications on a particular router fails, the other software applications on the other routers can make up for this. One of the primary advantages of these types of firewalls is in the ease of setup.

4. The Screened Host Configuration:

This type of firewall is actually a combination of different firewalls. In this specific configuration, a bastion host and a screening router are used. This combination is very effective in filtering the flow of data packets that are coming into the network infrastructure from the external environment. In this type of configuration, the bastion host could also serve as an application gateway and/or a router data packet screener. In a way, this is very similar to the dual-homed host configuration. With the screened cost configuration, only one network interface is required, and it does not a require a separate subnet in between the application gateway and the router. As a result, this makes the firewall much more flexible, but far less secure. The primary reason for this is that it is only relying upon one NIC, and it could be maliciously configured to gain unauthorized access to the more mission-critical aspects of the network infrastructure. Apart from this, there are also two other distinct disadvantages when using this approach to protect your web application:

 – It combines two firewalls into one, so if there is any sort of misconfiguration, both firewalls will be affected.
 – This configuration makes use of differing techniques for how the data packets will be filtered. For example, this type of configuration is operated typically at the network layer of the OSI model (which was examined

earlier in this chapter) and will simply block certain types of data packets based upon the network protocol that is being used, the port number, source IP address, and destination IP address. Also, the various port numbers work in the transport layer of the OSI model, thus offering yet another method for data packet filtering.

Finally, as you and your IT security staff determine the types of firewalls you need and the various configurations, it is very important that you do not develop the mentality that "more is better." In other words, just don't simply deploy 10 or 15 firewalls in the hopes that they will defend your web application server. There are two primary disadvantages with this:

- You are simply increasing the attack surface for the cyberattacker.
- You are spending a lot of money out of your precious IT funds.

Rather, as the CIO or CISO, you need to first conduct an assessment as to where the firewalls should be strategically placed, and from there, spend the money appropriately in order to procure and deploy them.

The Use of Intrusion Detection Systems

While the deployment and the implementation of firewalls is no doubt crucial to ensure the security of a web application server, other tools must be used as well in a multilayered approach. A business or a corporation simply cannot just depend upon a firewall to provide exclusive defense. If this were the case, then a cyberattacker could very easily break into a web application and cause all of sorts of malicious damage to not just the web application itself but everything that it is associated with it.

But by having multilayered approach, if the cyberattacker breaks through one line of defense, the chances become statistically much lower of he or she penetrating through the other layers. Thus, one of the best security tools that can be used in conjunction with a firewall is that of a network intrusion detection system (NIDS).

Understanding What a Network Intrusion Detection System Is

In technical terms, it can be defined as the following:

> It is a device that has been designed to detect for signs that a cyberattacker is attempting to breach a system in the network infrastructure and to alert the IT security staff that suspicious or anomalous behavior is taking place.

The NIDS inspects and examines all of the inbound as well as outbound port activity on a web application. By doing this, it looks for suspicious patterns that could indicate that a cyberattack is about to be launched or is currently underway.

For instance, if the NIDS determines that a series of data packets were sent to each port in a sequential fashion from the same source-based IP address, this is highly indicative that the network infrastructure is being maliciously scanned for any vulnerabilities and weaknesses that may exist.

Also, a key advantage of a NIDS is that it can quite easily and efficiently detect an abnormally huge influx of data packets from the same IP address in just a very short period of time. Actually, the primitive NIDS was just a hub. Then it became a network switch.

With this approach, once a data packet has traveled all the way from the end user's device to the server that is hosting the web application, it makes its way to the subnet to which the web application is connected to. Once this has been accomplished, the MAC address of the server is used to locate the server, and from that point onwards, the data packets would then be directed towards the server.

Thus, all of the web application servers on a particular subnet could see those particular data packets, and if the MAC address of the destination web application server did not match any other MAC addresses, the data packets would then be discarded.

This gave rise to the data packet sniffer (as discussed previously), but then people started to realize that if the contents of a data packet could be collected, they could also be analyzed in order to detect any malicious signs or abnormal network behavior.

Preemptive Blocking

This is also referred to in technical terms as banishment vigilance. The primary goal of a NIDS-based system is to prevent a malicious intrusion from occurring before it explodes into a large-scale cyberattack. This can be done in the early footprinting stages of a pending intrusion, then from there, blocking the IP address that is at the root of this malicious behavior. Although this may sound like an easy task to accomplish, it can actually be a very complex process to undertake.

The primary reason for this is that it can be quite difficult at times to determine and ascertain legitimate network traffic from malicious network traffic. This can result in an escalation of false positives. This occurs when the NIDS mistakenly identifies legitimate network traffic as anomalous behavior. If this were to happen, the NIDS would then shut down that flow of data packets to the web application server, no matter what.

It should be noted at this point the use of AI and ML tools are becoming of prime importance. Specifically, AI can be defined as follows:

> Artificial intelligence (AI) makes it possible for machines to learn from experience, adjust to new inputs and perform human-like tasks. Most AI examples that you hear about today – from chess-playing computers to self-driving cars – rely heavily on deep learning and natural language

processing. Using these technologies, computers can be trained to accomplish specific tasks by processing large amounts of data and recognizing patterns in the data.

Here are some of the important characteristics of artificial intelligence:

1. AI automates a process through repetitive learning and discovery through data: Artificial intelligence platforms perform very frequent, high-volume, computerized tasks reliably and without fatigue. For this type of automation, human inquiry is still essential to set up the system and ask the right questions.
2. AI adds intelligence to securing a web application: For example, automation, conversational platforms, bots, and smart machines can be combined with large amounts of information and data to greatly improve the security of a web application server.
3. AI adapts and learns through various progressive learning algorithms: AI finds structure and regularities in the information and data that are contained in the data packet so that the AI algorithm acquires a skill. The algorithm becomes a classifier or a predictor, in this case of a potential cyberattack. Also, the AI models adapt when given new data about the cyberthreat landscape. Back-propagation is an AI technique that allows the model to adjust, through training and added data, when the first answer is not quite right.
4. AI analyzes more and deeper data: Building a cyberthreat modeling system with five hidden layers was almost impossible a few years ago. All that has changed with incredible computer power and big data. You need lots of data to train deep learning models because these models learn directly from the data. The more data you can feed these models, the more accurate they become in predicting how a web application server might be affected by malicious data packet flows.
5. AI achieves incredible accuracy: This is done via using what is known as deep neural networks.

The following are the various components of artificial intelligence:

1. Machine Learning: This automates analytical model building. It uses methods from neural networks, statistics, operations research, and physics to find hidden insights in data without explicitly being programmed for where to look or what to conclude.
2. The Neural Network: This is a type of machine learning that is made up of interconnected units (like neurons) that process information by responding to external inputs,

relaying information between each unit. The process requires multiple passes at the data to find connections and derive meaning from undefined data.

3. Deep Learning:
This makes use of large neural networks with many layers of processing units, taking advantage of advances in computing power and improved training techniques to learn complex patterns in large amounts of information and data. Common applications include image and speech recognition.

4. Computer Vision:
This relies upon pattern recognition and deep learning to recognize what's in a picture or video. When machines can process, analyze, and understand images, they can capture images or videos in real time and interpret their surroundings. This can also be very helpful in creating a virtual, dynamic scene of a cyberthreat landscape.

Machine learning can be specifically defined as follows:

> The goal of machine learning is to understand the structure of the data and fit theoretical distributions to the data that are well understood. Machine learning has been developed based on the ability to use computers to probe the data for structure. The test for a machine learning model is the validation of error on new data, not a theoretical test that proves a null hypothesis. Because machine learning often uses an iterative approach to learn from data, the learning can be easily automated. Passes are run through the data until a robust pattern is found.

So as one can see from these definitions and concepts, the use of both machine learning and artificial intelligence can be a huge boon to the IT security staff when determining which alerts coming in from the firewalls and the NIDS are false positives and which data packets are malicious or not. It can take a human being many hours to accomplish these particular tasks, but with the use of both artificial intelligence and machine learning, this can be done within a matter of seconds.

This is especially crucial when the cyberthreat landscape is changing on literally a minute-by-minute basis. However, as noted, both artificial intelligence and machine learning tools require the use of live information and data feeds so that they can learn about the profiles from past threat vectors and predict those that could be harmful to a web application server.

Anomaly Detection

This technique makes use of specific software in order to detect intrusion attempts on the web application server and to alert the IT security staff when these types of incidents actually take place. With this, any type of activity that does not match the pattern of normal data traffic to the web application is thus noted and logged. This is achieved by comparing actual, observed activity against expected data packets to the web application server.

This kind of activity can also be referred to as a "traceback" because once an anomaly is detected, either the artificial intelligence or the machine learning tool tries to ascertain where this malicious activity first originated. Some of the ways in which a particular anomaly can be detected include the following:

- Threshold Monitoring:
  This process establishes a certain baseline of acceptable behavior and makes observations if any type of activity has actually exceeded the baseline that has been set forth. However, establishing what is deemed to be an acceptable level of risk to the web application server just based on this method can be quite challenging, because this involves much more of a qualitative judgment as to what the particular level of baseline should be, as opposed to using a quantitative-based approach.
- Resource Profiling:
  This methodology considers and measures the system-wide use of shared resources, and from there, historic profiles are thus created. This can be used to help determine any malicious or anomalous behavior that is taking place. But once again, since this is more of a macro-level key performance indicator (KPI) of a network infrastructure, false positives can be generated as well. For example, increased usage of a certain part of a network infrastructure may not necessarily mean that an attack is underway against a web application server; it just indicates that the web application in question is getting increased traction from the various end users that are trying to access it.
- Executable Profiling:
  This particular technique measures and quantifies how the various software packages in a web application server use the services that are available from it. But the key difference here is that it tracks those kinds and types of activities *that cannot be traced back to a particular end user.* This includes the cyberattacks of viruses, Trojan horses, worms, trapdoors, etc. This is accomplished by specifically profiling how web application server objects are accessed from both the internal confines of the network infrastructure and the data packet flow and network communications that are coming to it from the external environment. This allows for the NIDS to help confirm any type of cyberattack that could be a grave risk to the web application server.

Important NIDS Processes and Subcomponents

It is important to note that once a NIDS is used in conjunction with a firewall in order to secure a web application server using a multi-tiered approach, many processes and subcomponents are involved in order to ensure its efficient and effective operations. Examples of this include the following:

1. The Activity:
   This is that part of the data packet that is of primary interest to the firewall or NIDS.
2. The Administrator:
   This is the particular individual who is responsible for the overall security of the web application server.
3. The Sensor:
   This is a specific NIDS component that collects the information and data about the inflow of data packets to the web application server.
4. The Alert:
   This a certain message from the analyzer of the NIDS indicating that some sort "interesting" activity has been detected from within the network infrastructure.
5. The Manager:
   This is the management component of the NIDS.
6. The Notification:
   This is the process by which the NIDS alerts the IT security staff of the "interesting" activity that is taking place.
7. The Event:
   This is the specific occurrence that a suspicious or malicious activity is underway.
8. The Data Source:
   This is the raw information and data that are stored in the data packet.
9. The Active NIDS:
   This is also known as an intrusion prevention system (IPS). This type of system will stop any and all network communications flow to the web application server that is deemed to be malicious or suspicious in nature.
10. The Passive NIDS:
    This system just logs all network activity coming into the web application server.
11. The HIDS:
    This stands for a host-based intrusion detection system. As its name implies, it only monitors just one subnet of the network infrastructure.
12. The HIPS:
    This stands for a host-based intrusion prevention system, and this type of system monitors all of the subnets of the entire network infrastructure.

The Use of VPNs to Protect a Web Application Server

VPNs are now becoming a very fast and very popular way for an end user to connect from his or her device to a web application server. At one time, this kind of technology was very expensive and only the Fortune 500 companies could afford to deploy it. But as the technology has quickly advanced and matured over time, the price of it has greatly come down, and in fact, a small to medium sized business (SMB) can even conduct a basic Google search to see which type of VPN will work best for them, pay on a subscription basis, and download and deploy it in a few minutes.

A VPN can be specifically defined as follows:

> A virtual private network (VPN) is a software application that creates a safe and encrypted connection over a less secure network, such as the public internet. A VPN works by using the shared public infrastructure while maintaining privacy through security procedures and tunneling protocols. In effect, the protocols, by encrypting data at the sending end and decrypting it at the receiving end, send the data through a 'tunnel' that cannot be 'entered' by data that is not properly encrypted. An additional level of security involves encrypting not only the data, but also the originating and receiving network addresses.

As one can see from this definition, a virtual private network creates a private network connection over the Internet in order to create a highly secure connection between the web application server and the device of the end user that is accessing it. Instead of using a dedicated connection, which can be easily detected by a data packet sniffer (such as that of an unencrypted Wi-Fi connection), the VPN makes use of what are known as virtual connections specifically routed through the Internet from the end user's device to the web application server.

The rest of this subsection is devoted to the VPN and how it can be specifically used to protect not only the lines of communication but the flow of data packets to the web application server.

The Basics of VPN Technology

In order to make this as seamless as possible, the VPN must literally emulate a direct network Internet connection, like those that can be publicly accessed. In other words, a VPN must be able to provide the same level of access as well as the exact same level of security that a fully encrypted, public Internet connection would provide (this is, of course, assuming it has been configured in this fashion).

In order to initiate this so-called "point to point" link, the data packets in the lines of communication are encapsulated, or wrapped, into a different header that provides the specific routing information in order for the data packets to reach the web application server from the end user's device, and vice versa. Thus, as stated previously, a virtual network connection is then established between these two end points. It is important to keep in mind that even the data packets receive an extra layer of encrypted protection as well.

Think of it this way: a VPN literally just piggybacks off of existing Internet connections in order to establish the second line of communication flow that is invisible and encrypted to the outside world.

The Virtual Private Network Protocols that are Used to Secure a Web Application Server

In today's cybersecurity world, numerous virtual private network protocols are used, and they are detailed as follows:

1. The PPTP:
   This is an acronym that stands for Point to Point Tunneling Protocol. This is actually a specific tunneling protocol that makes use of an older network connection protocol known as Point to Point Protocol (PPP) for short. PPTP enables the data packets to be encapsulated (or encrypted) over the IP protocol and thus have the ability to be forwarded to any IP-based network in which the web application server is interfaced, or linked to. Point to Point Tunneling Protocol is actually one of the first and oldest forms of VPN connections to be created. It made its first public appearance in 1996 by a consortium known as the PPTP Forum. Although PPTP is still widely used today, one of its main benefits is that it operates at layer 2 of the OSI model (as reviewed earlier in this chapter), which is the data link layer. Another primary advantage of the PPTP is that it can support the encrypted transmission of older forms of data packets, such as those of IPX, NetBEUI, and others. It is important to note at this point that PPTP supports two kinds of tunneling mechanisms, which are as follows:
   - Voluntary Tunneling:
     In this type of scenario, the device of the end user that is attempting to establish a connection with the web application server first connects to the network backbone of an Internet service provider (ISP), and from this point, the VPN is then launched in order to create the secure PPTP session. With this setup, the end user actually selects the type and level of encryption and authentication that he or she wishes to use, hence, the name.
   - Compulsory Tunneling:
     In this type of configuration, the web application automatically selects the encryption and authentication protocols that are to be used.

How PPTP Sessions are Authenticated

Although establishing the lines of secure communication between the device of the end user and the web application server (which is primarily done through encryption) is of paramount importance, so is authenticating the end user. This is particularly true in those instances where the web application would also consist of an e-commerce component, in which financial information and data are exchanged and where credit card information is stored.

There are two separate authentication tools to do this under PPTP, and they are as follows:

1. EAP:

   This is an acronym that stands for Extensible Authentication Protocol. This was specifically designed to work with PPTP and provides the framework and baseline for several other different authentication protocols to be used as well. This includes the use of RSA tokens, and the public key infrastructure (this will be reviewed in much more detail in Chapter 2, which is about cryptography).

2. CHAP:

   This is an acronym that stands for Challenge Handshake Authentication Protocol. This technique is actually a three-way handshaking process in order to fully authenticate the end user. Here is how this process specifically works:

   – Once the network lines of communication have been established between the device of the end user and the web application server, the sever actually sends a challenge message to the device of the end user.
   – This device in turn responds to this challenge by transmitting a specific value which has been computed using a one-way mathematical hashing function.
   – In return, the web application server checks this response against the hash value that it has computed, and if these two values match up, the end user is then fully authenticated into the web application server. But if the values do match up, the network connection that has been established between the device of the end user and the web application server is immediately terminated.

   A primary advantage with this technique is that this three-way handshaking process is refreshed on a daily basis, thus creating new hash values on a dynamic and real-time basis.

How Layer 2 Tunneling Protocol (L2TP) Sessions are Authenticated

L2TP is often viewed as an enhanced extension of PPTP because it is often used with a VPN. L2TP operates at the data link layer of the OSI model. In fact, the L2TP protocol is very often used in conjunction with the IPSec protocol (this will be reviewed in more detail later in this chapter) in order to provide for a robust and secure VPN.

L2TP supports the following authentication mechanisms:

- MS-CHAP:

    This authentication mechanism was created by Microsoft exclusively for the Windows Server operating systems. Its primary objective is to further the local area networks (LANs) upon which a web application server may reside, as well as to integrate hashing and encryption mathematical algorithms in client-server–based network topologies. But there are some exclusive functionalities of MS-CHAP, which are as follows:
    - It is only designed to be interoperable in a Windows-based networking enterprise.
    - Cleartext and passwords that can be reverse-engineered are not supported
    - It provides for authenticator-based retry and automatic password changing mechanisms.
    - It possesses what is known as a reason for failure code system, in that certain values are returned if certain data packets do not reach the web application server, for whatever reason, if the authenticator has failed. These are a specific set of codes that only a Windows Server operating system can interpret, thus providing for a specific reason for the failure of the authenticator.

How Password Authentication Protocol (PAP) Sessions are Authenticated

PAP is actually one of the most basic and rudimentary forms of authentication that currently exists for use with a VPN. In this case, the password of the end user is transmitted to the subnet in which the particular web application server belongs and it is compared to a table (or listing) of legitimate passwords. PAP has two very distinct disadvantages in terms of security:

- The password that is transmitted from the device of the end user and the web application server is sent over in a cleartext format.
- It is meant to work with HTTP and not the Hypertext Transport Protocol-Secure (HTTPS) protocol.

How Shiva Password Authentication Protocol (SPAP) Sessions are Authenticated

SPAP is viewed more as a closed-source version of PAP. Although the password is fully encrypted, its main disadvantage is that it is highly prone to what are known as playback attacks. This occurs when a cyberattacker records the flow of network communication between the device of the end user and the web application server and retransmits it again in order to gain unauthorized access to the web application server. The primary reason for this is that the levels of encryption that are afforded with this specific protocol could be reverse-engineered, given that the cyberattacker has the right set of tools to do this.

How Kerberos Protocol Sessions are Authenticated

This specific protocol was developed at the Massachusetts Institute of Technology (MIT) and was given this particular name in reference to the three-headed dog that protected the fortified gates to the kingdom of Hades. Kerberos specifically works by sending messages back and forth between the device of the end user and the web application server, and even vice versa. Its strongest advantage is that the password of the end user is actually never sent in transit. Instead, the username is transmitted back and forth. From this point, the web application server then looks up the stored hash digest of the end user's password and uses a private key (this will be addressed in much more detail in Chapter 2) to encrypt any data that is transmitted back and forth between the device of the end user and the web application server.

At this point, the device of the end user uses that same private key in order to decrypt, or unlock, the data that has been sent to it. The key point to remember here is that if the end user types in the wrong password, this data will never be decrypted. This entire process occurs with what is known as the User Data Protocol (UDP) for short. Here is a detailed overview of how all of this transpires.

First, after the username is transmitted to the authentication server (AS) that is hosted on the web application server, the web application server will then use a specific hash digest of the password that is protected by the private key. Two messages are sent at this point:

- Message A: This contains the Client/Ticket Granting Service (TGS) session, which is encrypted by the private key.
- Message B: This contains the Ticket Granting Ticket (TGT) that consists of the following:
  - The username of the end user
  - The network address of the device (of the end user) that is connected
  - The validity period

Once the device of the end user attempts to decrypt Message A with the private key, the password that is in that data packet will be compared to what the end user has typed in. If the two passwords match up, the decryption process continues; if not, the session is immediately terminated. Assuming that the two passwords do correspond exactly, there is yet another message process, which is as follows:

- Message C: This consists of the TGT from Message B and the username of the end user that is requesting access to the web application server

■ Message D: This consists of the authenticator (which resides on the web application server) and the username of the end user, as well as the timestamp when the communication to the web application is requested by the end user

Once Message C and Message D have been received by the TGS, the TGS then attempts to obtain Message B via both Message C and Message B. It should be noted that Message B is decrypted using the TGS private key. This is known specifically as the client/TGS session key. By making use of this key, the TGS then decrypts Message D (which is the authenticator), and at this point, the following two messages are then transmitted:

■ Message E: This is a client-to-server–based ticket that includes the following:
  – The username of the end user
  – The network address of the device (of the end user) that is connected
  – The validity period
  – The client/server session key that is encrypted using the private key
■ Message F: This is the client/server session key that is further encrypted by the client TGS session that was established earlier.

Once these two messages have been received by the TGS, the device of the end user that is attempting to make a connection with the web application server can now be 100% authenticated to the service server (SS) that also resides upon the web application server. Once this has been established, two new messages are sent:

■ Message E: The content of this particular message is encrypted using the SS private key.
■ Message G: This is a brand-new authenticator (which also resides on the web application server), which consists of the username of the end user and the timestamp when the communication to the web application was requested by the end user.

The SS then decrypts the ticket (which is Message E) by making use of its private key to retrieve the client/server session key. By making use of this same key, the SS also decrypts the authenticator (which resides on the web application server) and then transmits the final message:

■ Message H: This is the timestamp that is found in the authenticator, as previously described.

The device of the end user then decrypts Message H by making use of the client/server key (as also previously described) and checks if the timestamp is correct. If this is confirmed, then the end user can trust the validity of the web application server and start requesting the various services that are available from it.

How IPSec Protocol Sessions are Authenticated

IPSec is an acronym that stands for Internet Security Protocol. This is what is used primarily today in VPNs. IPSec is used in conjunction with the IP protocol to add an extra layer of high-level security to TCP/IP-based network communications. IPSec was created and developed by the Internet Engineering Task Force (IETF). It has two separate and distinct levels of encryption:

■ Transport mode: This is when the entire data packet is encrypted, except for its header. What this means is that the source address, the destination address, and the data that is contained in the header remain unencrypted.
■ Tunnel mode: This encrypts the rest of the data packet, which is the header and the data that resides in it.

It is important to note here that IPSec is a single key-based encryption technology, and it also offers two extra protocols:

1. The Authentication Header (AH):
   This protocol provides yet another mechanism solely for the purposes of authentication. It assures the following:
   – The integrity of the data that is contained in the header of the data packet (this is verified by HMAC-MD5 and/or HMAC-SHA)
   – The authentication level of the origin of the data (this is verified by making use of a private key)
   – A replay protection service.
2. The Encapsulating Security Payload (ESP):
   This ensures optimal levels for data confidentiality and authentication when the VPN is first established. It can operate in the following modes:
   – Confidentiality only
   – Authentication only
   – A combination of both

It is important to note here as well that there are types of protocols that make IPSec the tool of choice for a VPN. One of these is known as the Internet Key Exchange (IKE) for short. This is used to help fortify the existing security functionalities that a VPN has to offer. For example, a secure association is created by the two endpoints of a VPN tunnel, and this ultimately will determine what information and data get encrypted and authenticated.

With regard to this, the following variables are taken into consideration:

■ What data packets will be encrypted?
■ What specific protocol will be used for the public key infrastructure (PKI; see Chapter 2)?
■ What specific protocol will be used for authentication purposes?

The answers to these questions are ultimately determined by the two endpoints of the VPN and are stored in a specialized database called the security association (SA). Another key protocol that is used is the Internet Security Association and Key Management (ISAKMP).

Here is a detailed overview of just how the IPSec authentication and key exchange process works:

1. The first exchange between the two VPN endpoints establishes the technical aspects of the security policy that the VPN will use.
2. The initiator then suggests the various encryption and authentication algorithms that can be used for the VPN.
3. The responder decides on the specific algorithms that will be used.
4. The second exchange between the two VPN endpoints passes on what are known as the Diffie-Hellman public keys (this will also be covered in Chapter 2).
5. These public keys will then be used to encrypt the data packets that will be sent between the two endpoints of the VPN.
6. The third exchange between the two endpoints of the VPN then authenticates the Internet Security Association and Key Management session, and this process is technically known as the main mode.
7. Once this step has been initiated, the IPSec-based negotiation is then triggered (this is specifically known as the quick mode).
8. The quick mode then further negotiates the SA for the level of encryption that will be used and does all of the key management for the IPSec protocol.
9. Finally the secure connection between the endpoints of the VPN is firmly established, and the transmission and flow of data packets between the device of the end user and the web application (and vice versa) is started and continues until the VPN is no longer needed.

How SSL Protocol Sessions are Authenticated

SSL is an acronym that stands for Secure Sockets Layer. It is also commonly referred to as Transport Layer Security (TLS). These are protocols that have been designed exclusively for web applications, the servers that house them, and for VPNs. Here is the process as to how it is used:

1. The device of the end user transmits to the web application server the type of SSL that is being used, the specific cipher-based settings, and the data packets that will be transmitted.
2. In return, the web application server sends its own set of this same information back to the device of the end user in order to establish the baseline, or profile, that will be needed to establish a secure connection.

3. The device of the end user then uses this information to confirm the "identity" of the web application server, taking into account the following parameters:
   - If the issuer of the SSL or TLS certificate originates from a trusted certificate authority
   - The expiration date of the SSL or TLS certificate
   - If the SSL or TLS has been revoked before

   If for some reason the web application server cannot be positively identified, then a secure connection cannot be guaranteed. But the end user still has the option of continuing onto the next step.
4. Assuming that a secure connection can actually be established, the device of the end user then transmits to the web application a specialized private key.
5. If the web application server accepts this private key, the device of the end user then transmits over its SSL or TSL certificate.
6. Based upon this, the web application server will attempt to authenticate the device of the end user. If this cannot be done, the network lines of communication between the two are then terminated. But if this can be done (meaning the device of the end user can be authenticated), the web application server will decrypt the private key that was originally sent over to it.
7. From this, a "master secret" is then formulated in order to establish a pair of session keys. These are "symmetric" based keys that are then used to encrypt and decrypt the data packets that are being sent from the device of the end user to the web application server (and vice versa).
8. Once these symmetric-based keys have been received by the device of the end user, all of the data packets that will be transmitted are then 100% confirmed to be encrypted as they traverse their way across the network line of communication from the device of the end user to the web application server (and vice versa).
9. In return, the web application will also confirm that any data packets that are transmitted from it will also be 100% encrypted.

How to Assess the Current State of Security of a Web Application Server

Whenever one thinks of conducting a security assessment, a deep and focused cybersecurity assessment probably comes to mind, in particular, penetration testing and threat hunting.

With penetration testing, the goal is to break down the walls of defense from the external environment going to the network infrastructure of the business or corporation. The primary objective here is to unearth any known security-related vulnerabilities and weaknesses and, of course, to provide remediation to them immediately.

With threat hunting, the primary goal is to break down the walls of defense starting internally with the network infrastructure, and from there, going into the external environment. The objectives of threat hunting are the same as penetration testing, but in reverse. The objective is to see if there are any covert pieces of malware that could exist from within the network infrastructure and determine how they got there in the first place from the external environment.

Penetration testing and threat hunting will be covered in Chapter 3 and Chapter 4, respectively. But there is yet another methodology that can be used to gauge the level of security as it relates to the web application in question and the server that it resides upon. This is known as a risk assessment and offers a more quantitative approach and utilizes various rating factors in order to determine just how much at risk the web application and its server face. We will turn to this next.

Important Risk Assessment Methodologies and How They Relate to Web Application Security

Single Loss Expectancy (SLE)

This methodology examines, or quantifies, what the exact impact will be for a single loss that could occur within the network infrastructure of a business or a corporation. This is simply calculated by multiplying the asset value (AV) by the exposure factor (EF). The latter reflects how much value could be lost if the web application server is hit by a single cyberattack, whether it is large or small.

Mathematically, it is represented as follows:

$$SLE = AV \times EF$$

The Annualized Loss Expectancy (ALE)

This methodology can be viewed as an extension of the one just described, but rather than looking at it from the standpoint of just one cyberattack affecting the web application server at one particular instance, the annualized loss expectancy examines it from the perspective of one year. This considers a new kind of variable, known as the annual rate of occurrence (ARO).

Mathematically, it is represented as follows:

$$ALE = SLE \times ARO$$

The Residual Risk

This methodology reflects how much security risk a web application still faces even after all of the known and unknown risks have been taken into consideration. It considers the following variables:

■ Mitigation: This refers how many steps that you and your IT security staff have taken to protect the web application server.

■ Avoidance: This means that there is, on a theoretical basis, no security risk that is posed to the web application server.
■ Transference: This refers to shifting the risk that is faced by the web application to another entity. A prime example of this is cybersecurity insurance. For example, if the web application and the server that it resides upon have been destroyed, the business or corporation will then file a claim with the respective insurance company. As a result, the insurance company then assumes the risk, because that entity will then have to process the claim and issue the funds.
■ Acceptance: This is the statistical probability that the risk of a cyberattack to a web application is extremely remote, and in fact, the cost of taking preventative measures exceeds the financial impact that a cyberattack could pose to the business or corporation.

How to Evaluate the Security Risk that is Posed to the Web Application and its Server

This involves assigning various numeric values of risk that the web application server faces. It includes examining the following variables:

■ The particular level of attractiveness of the web application and the server that it resides upon to the cyberattacker
■ The nature of the sensitivity of the PII that is stored in the web application
■ The level of security that is already in place for the web application server

Each of these variables, in turn, is then assigned a specific numerical value as follows:

1. The Level of Attractiveness:
   This will receive a rating of 1 if the web application has no value to the cyberattacker, but will receive a value of 10 if it is very attractive to the cyberattacker.
2. The Sensitivity Nature of the PII:
   This will receive a rating of 1 if there is no PII stored on the web application, but will receive a value of 10 if there is PII stored on the web application.
3. The Level of Security:
   This will receive a rating of 10 if there are layers of security to guard the web application server, but will receive a value of 1 if there are no layers of security to guard the web application server.

In order to compute the specific value of risk that is posed to the web application and the server that it resides upon, the following mathematical formula is used, considering the previously mentioned variables:

The level of attractiveness + The sensitivity nature of the PII − The level of security = The risk posed to the web application

Once this value has been computed, it can then be applied to the following rating scale:

The Value That Has Been Computed	The Level of Risk to the Web Application
1	No Impact
2–3	Slight Impact
4–5	Medium Impact
6–7	Major Impact
8–9	Significant Impact
10	Catastrophic Impact

How to Conduct the Initial Security Assessment on the Web Application

In the last section of this chapter, we reviewed some key risk assessment models that you should take into consideration when assessing the level of risk that your web application(s) and the server(s) they reside upon. Once you have completed this key step, the next one is to actually conduct the initial assessment. Remember, this can get quite complex; therefore, it is crucial to keep this as clear and simple as possible so that other key stakeholders in the business or corporation will be able to understand and proactively act upon it.

In order to accomplish this, there is yet another methodology called the Five Ps, and they are as follows:

■ Patches
■ Ports
■ Protection
■ Probing
■ Physical

They are now examined in further detail in this section.

1. Patches:
   As most cybersecurity professionals can attest, applying software patches and updates (even the firmware) to the web application is one of the most fundamental and even crucial aspects that you and your IT security staff should be embarking upon. In this regard, you should confirm that there

is a documented policy in place that outlines in detail how often software upgrades and patches should be checked for at the vendor site, when they should be downloaded, the schedule for deploying them, and how they should be implemented. In fact, this process should be a key component of the overall security policy of the business or corporation. In terms of the web application, this includes the following:

- The operating system of the web application server
- The database
- The source code
- The Internet browsers that are used to access the web application from within the business or corporation
- The front end of the web application

In conducting this part of the initial assessment, you need to first confirm that all of the current software patches, upgrades, and firmware have all been deployed onto the web application server. Once this has been confirmed, the next step is to set up a schedule for regular audits in order to make sure that the software patches, upgrades, and firmware are checked for and deployed in the manner that has been explicitly set forth by the security policy.

2. Ports:

It is important to keep in mind that any and all types of network communications between the device of the end user and the web application server keep open ports by mistake. Thus, this becomes a prime target for the cyberattacker in order to launch virus- and malware-based cyberattacks against the web application server. Usually, those ports numbered 1 through 1024 are the well-known ports that are used by most businesses and corporations. Therefore, the cyberattacker will go after some less commonly used port in order to launch their threat vectors. Therefore, it is very important to conduct a complete and thorough audit of all of the ports in the entire network infrastructure and determine those ports that are not currently being used. Once this has been ascertained, it is absolutely crucial that these are shut down immediately, so that they do not become a backdoor for the cyberattacker. The only ports that should remain open are those that are currently being used by some sort of associated service on the web application server. Remember, do not simply rely upon your firewall and/or router to filter the flow of malicious data packets that are inbound to the network infrastructure. The primary reason for this is that firewalls and routers can also be a prime target for the cyberattacker. Also, just as in the case of software upgrades, patches, and firmware, a regular schedule must be established in order to check for and shut down any unused ports. This affords the business or corporation a layered security approach, not just a perimeter-based one (this would be the case if you solely rely upon your firewalls and/or routers).

3. Protection:

As its name implies, this part of the initial assessment involves making sure that the entire network infrastructure is protected and well-fortified, using the latest security software applications and hardware. This includes the following:

- Firewalls and routers are put into place (especially making use of those that are stateful packet inspection based).
- Antivirus and antimalware software packages are deployed onto the web application server.
- Network intrusion devices are also deployed.
- Proxy servers are being used (this will mask all of the IP addresses that are internal to the network infrastructure).
- All lines of network communications from the web application server to the external environment are encrypted and made secure through use of a VPN.

It is also equally important to conduct regular security audits (at least once a quarter) in order to make sure that these functionalities are fully optimized in order fortify the lines of defense of the business or corporation.

4. Physical:

Apart from hardening your entire network infrastructure and all of the IT assets that reside within it, you must also equally ensure that the business or corporation has deployed and implemented equal amounts of security from the physical access entry perspective as well. This simply means that only authorized personnel are able to physically to access the data center where the web application server resides. This should be a key and fundamental of your overall security policy as well. Because so much attention is paid to network security, this is an often-forgotten aspect. This realm of security also includes providing strong layers of physical security to other aspects as well, such as backup tapes and other key documentation as it relates to the web application and the server that it resides upon. Also, access to any type of security tools should be highly restricted. This includes the routers, firewalls, switches, hubs, network intrusion devices, etc. Any company devices that are issued to employees should have some sort of mark engraved into them, so that they can easily be identified, and they should be inventoried and accounted for on a quarterly basis. Just like in network security, you must also implement multiple layers of security when it comes to physical access entry. In this aspect, the use of biometric technology, such as hand geometry recognition, iris recognition, and fingerprint recognition, is a robust modality for any business or corporation to implement. These techniques should be used for the main entry access both externally and internally within the organization. Also, keep in mind that by maintaining strong levels of physical access entry security, this will even help mitigate the risks of an insider attack from occurring. These are very difficult to detect, and even a legitimate employee that has access to a web application can cause serious damage to it. Therefore, in order to be proactive about this, the organization must maintain a 24 × 7 × 365 confidential hotline so that any suspicious activity can be reported immediately.

5. Probing:

This typically involves conducting a deep scan of the network infrastructure in order to discover any unknown security weaknesses and gaps. In this instance, this is where penetration testing and threat hunting become absolutely critical (these topics will be covered much more extensively in Chapters 3 and 4, respectively). Network infrastructure probing on a macro level typically involves the following:

   – Port scanning: This typically involves scanning all of the network ports that are most commonly used. But in order to conduct a much more thorough search, all of the ports that reside in your network infrastructure should be scanned.
   – Enumerating: This is where either the penetration testing or threat hunting teams adopt the mind-set of a real-world cyberattacker and compromise such items as employee access accounts, shared resources and folders, printers, and other hardware items associated with the web application server.
   – Vulnerability assessment: This is the use of any and perhaps even all available network sniffing and probing tools in order to assess both known and unknown vulnerabilities. This is typically decided upon before the threat hunting and penetration teams engage in their exercises.

Techniques Used by Cyberattackers against the Web Application and Web Application Server

In this section, we provide a high-level overview of some of the major techniques that the cyberattacker of today uses when it comes to launching their particular threat vectors. It is important to keep in mind that in the cyberthreat landscape of today, the cyberattacker is becoming much more covert and stealthier in the ways that they hack. In the past, the primary goal of the cyberattacker was to steal as much confidential information and data as they could about their victims. In other words, not much forethought was given into planning the actual attack. The main intention was a "try and get all" effort within the first shot. This has also been referred to as "smash and grab" campaigns. But as mentioned, this kind of mentality has now completely shifted into the opposite direction. For example, the cyberattacker of today is now taking their time in researching and profiling their victims.

They are not necessarily just targeting everything at random, but rather, they choose their victims with deliberate forethought. They take as much time as needed to study all of the vulnerabilities and weaknesses, and once they are ready, they then "move in for the kill." But a key differentiating factor now is that rather than using the "try and get all" approach, the goal of the cyberattacker is to move in slowly, in small increments.

The primary goal here is to stay inside the confines of the victim organization for as long as possible, going unnoticed. But at this point, it is now very important to distinguish what the terms hacking and attacking really mean, as a there is a distinct differentiation between the two, which are specifically defined as follows:

- Hacker: "In computing, a hacker is any skilled computer expert that uses their technical knowledge to overcome a problem."
- Attacker: "In computer and computer networks an attack is any attempt to destroy, expose, alter, disable, steal or gain unauthorized access to or make unauthorized use of an asset. Thus, an attacker is the individual or organization performing these malicious activities."

Thus, as one can see from these two definitions, a hacker is an individual (or group of individuals) whose primary interest is that of just sheer curiosity. He or she has particular expertise in a certain area of IT and wants to apply that in order to learn more about what they are targeting, especially about its security weaknesses and vulnerabilities.

In fact, there three distinct types of hacker, which are as follows:

- The white hat hacker: This is an individual (or a team of individuals) who is hacking for ethical and lawful purposes, with written and explicit consent from the owners of the targeted victim. This is the penetration tester.
- The black hat hacker: This is an individual (or a team of individuals) who is hacking *for unethical and illegal* purposes.
- The gray hat hacker: This is an individual (or a team of individuals) who lies in between the other two types of hacking. In other words, sometimes they are ethical and law abiding, but other times they are not.

Thus, an attacker is an individual who is out to cause harm or damage (such as stealing confidential information and data) for the prime motivation of financial gain once they have learned all about the particular system's weaknesses and vulnerabilities. So in reality, a cyberattacker can be considered a cyberhacker at first, and as they launch their attack, they are then an official cyberattacker.

The Techniques Used by the Cyberhacker

This subsection details some of the key techniques that are used by the cyberhacker. The subsection after this one will then explore those techniques that are used by the cyberattacker.

1. Passive Searching:

   In most cases, the cyberhacker will start here. In this technique, the goal is to gather as much as information and data as possible about the target system and does not involve any sort of direction or interaction with it by the cyberhacker. Note in this situation, we use the term "target" and not "victim," as there is no damage or harm that is being caused yet. In order to accomplish this task, the cyberhacker will use various searching tools (examples of this include www.netcraft.com and www.archive.org) in order to get this information and data. The cyberhacker may even conduct some social engineering exercises to a very limited degree in order to learn about the people that are associated with the target that is being studied.

2. Active Scanning:

   As its name implies, this technique requires that the cyberhacker have a direct connection with the intended target to some degree in order to get the information and data that they seek. Examples of typical scans include the following:

   – Port scanning: This involves conducting a deep scan to see what ports are open on the web application server. The port number typically reveals the specific services that each port is actually using. In this regard, one of the most widely used tools to conduct a port scan is Nmap. It is a downloadable tool that is available from www.nmap.org. By using this particular tool, various "flags" can be implemented in order to mark those pieces of information and data that the cyberhacker is seeking. The flags in Nmap include the following:
     - -0: Operating System Detection
     - -sP: The Ping Scan
     - sT: The TCP Connection Scan
     - -sS: The SYN Scan
     - -sF: The FIN Scan
     - -sN: The NULL Scan
     - -sU: The UDP Scan
     - -s0: The Protocol Scan
     - -sA: The ACK Scan
     - -sW: The Windows Scan
     - -sR: The RPC Scan
     - -sL: The List/DNS Scan
     - -sI: The Idle Scan
     - -Po: The Don't Ping
     - -PT: The TCP Ping
     - -PS: The TCP and ICMP Pings
     - -PM: The ICMP Netmask
     - -oN: The Normal Output
     - -oX: The XML Output
     - -oG: The Greppable Output
     - -oA: The All Output

- Vulnerability assessment: In this case, the cyberhacker is trying to determine what the security weaknesses and gaps are in the intended target. Some of the favored utilities that are used to accomplish this task include the following:
    - The Ping scan: This is a specialized scan that sends various Ping-based ICMP data packets to the IP address of the intended target in order to determine what ports are open (as just discussed). The main drawback with this specific utility is that many types of firewalls and routers block the ICMP data packets. For those web application servers that make use of the Linux operating system, the Traceroute utility is used (it is also referred to as "tracert" from the command line prompt).
- The connect scan: This type of utility makes a full and complete connection to the target system by connecting with the specific IP address that is associated with any given port.
- The SYN scan: This utility examines how the network connectivity works with the intended target system. In order to do this, an exchange of data packets is transmitted from the cyberhacker to the web application server (and vice versa). This is how it is accomplished:
    - The device that is used by the cyberhacker sends over a SYN Flag to the web application server (which is also the intended target in this scenario).
    - The web application then sends back a SYN-ACK Flag. Essentially, the web application is saying to the device of the cyberhacker that a connection can be established between the two.
    - The device of the cyberhacker then sends back an ACK Flag, which acknowledges the connection to the web application server.
3. Enumerating:
    This is when the cyberhacker simply wants to find out what the specific shared resources and shared folders are on the intended target (which is also the web application server).
4. Manual Scanning:
    This is when the cyberhacker chooses to examine the target system using traditional methods. In this particular instance, the telnet command is often used, which makes use of port 23. In order to perform this kind of manual scan, the cyberhacker merely launches a command line and from there enters the following command:

```
telnet [IP address OR Domain Name] [PORT NUMBER]
```

After this command has been executed, the cyberhacker can then execute the following command to determine what kind of operating system and related services the web application server is using:

```
HEAD / HTTP/ 1.0
```

Techniques Used by the Cyberattacker

This section provides an overview of some of the major types of threat vectors that can be launched against the target system (which is the web application server) once enough vulnerabilities and weaknesses have been discovered.

1. Circumventing the Password:

   Obviously, one of the most sought after "crown jewels" is the password of the victim. With this, just about any harm or damage can be done, ranging from financial loss all the way to identity theft. But there are also ways that a cyberattacker can launch a threat vector against the target system, bypassing the password entirely. Here is how it can be done using a Windows-based web application server:

   – Obtain a Linux operating system boot disk.
   – Boot this CD.
   – Once this has been accomplished, locate and access the specific NTFS volume by using the following commands:

   ```
   Fdisk -1 | grep NTFS
   Mkdir -p /mnt/windows
   Mount -t ntfs-3g /dev/sda1 /mnt/windows
   ```

   – Once this has been accomplished, you can move over to the Windows system 32 directory structure to create a copy of what is known as the magnify application by issuing the following commands:

   ```
   Cd /mnt/windows/Windows/System32
   Mv magnify.exe magnify.bck
   ```

   – Then make a copy of the cmd.exe (this is the command prompt) and from here, change its respective name to magnify.exe, by issuing the following command:

   ```
   Cp cm.exe magnify.exe and reboot
   ```

   – Now you can reboot into Windows and log into the Windows-based web application server by selecting the Accessibility and Magnifier options.

2. SQL Injection:

   SQL is an acronym that stands for Structured Query Language and is still one of the most widely forms of threat vectors used by the cyberattacker. The prime target here is the login screen of the web application, in which the end user must enter in a username and password. This combination is, of course, checked against a database of all issued usernames and passwords in order to confirm that what has been entered by the end user is actually valid. Here is how this can attack can be simulated:

— When creating the username and password database, the SQL code that has been used to create the actual web application is found in quotation marks in order to separate it from the source code that has been used to create the web application, demonstrated as follows:

```
'SELECT * FROM tblUsers WHERE USERNAME = ' " +
txtUsername.Text +' AND PASSWORD = ' " +
txtPassword.Text + " ' "
```

— If the username of "admin" and the password "password" is entered into the login screen, the following SQL command is then created:

```
SELECT * FROM tblUsers WHERE USERNAME = 'admin' and
PASSWORD = 'password'
```

— In order to initiate a SQL injection attack, the cyberattacker issues a command just after 'password', which is as follows:

```
'password' OR x=x
```

— This command then creates the following query:

```
SELECT * FROM tblUsers WHERE USERAME = 'admin' and
PASSWORD = 'password' OR X=X
```

This query then tells the SQL based database as well as the Web application to allow for a malicious login, X=X

— In order to delete records in a SQL database, the cyberattacker issues the following command:

```
X'; DROP TABLE users; - -
```

— In order to hack into a SQL database that consists of email addresses, the cyberattacker issues the following command:

```
X' UPDATE members SET email = 'me@somewhere.net'
WHERE email = 'somebody@example.com'
```

It is important to note that that these SQL-based commands are only the basic ones. They can get far more complex, covert, and stealthy, based upon the skill level of the cyberattacker.

3. Cross-Site Scripting (XSS):

This type of cyberattack deals specifically with the HTML-based pages that have been created for the specific web application in question. It can be defined specifically as follows:

Cross-Site Scripting (XSS) attacks are a type of injection, in which malicious scripts are injected into otherwise benign and trusted websites. XSS attacks occur when an attacker uses a web application to send malicious code, generally in the form of a browser side script, to a different end user. Flaws that allow these attacks to succeed are quite widespread and occur anywhere a web application uses input from a user within the output it generates without validating or encoding it.

An attacker can use XSS to send a malicious script to an unsuspecting user. The end user's browser has no way to know that the script should not be trusted, and will execute the script. Because it thinks the script came from a trusted source, the malicious script can access any cookies, session tokens, or other sensitive information retained by the browser and used with that site. These scripts can even rewrite the content of the HTML page.

In simpler terms, the cyberattacker inserts a malicious-based client-side script into the HTML-based pages of the web application that the end user accesses. In turn, the original functionality of the web application is rendered useless, and thus the end user is redirected to spoofed website that looks exactly like the real web application.

Network Security and Its Relevance for Web Apps

It seems as though at least once a month (and sometimes more commonly) a major story occurs in the news about a significant data breach. Hundreds of millions (if not billions) of pieces of information are compromised by attackers – and these are only the *major* breaches. Between high-profile misconfigurations of cloud data sources, the exposure of data due to unencrypted in-flight data, and attackers tricking users into giving up their information to look-alike web apps, the dangers are varied and serious.

For the purposes of this book, we'll talk about network security from two perspectives. First, we'll talk about data confidentiality – the security related to the actual transmission of data between different aspects of a system – as it pertains to the network. Any time that your application is communicating with a client, server, database, etc., these are places where communications will traverse a network. Any time such traversal happens, it is possible that data can be viewed (passive) or intercepted (active) by third parties.

Second, we'll discuss site validity – the concept that users need to be able to trust that your web app is authentic. I believe that these two topics *must* be combined, as having one without the other leaves web app developers with a dangerous blind spot to many major attack vectors.

Data Confidentiality

Data confidentiality, as mentioned earlier, is security related to the actual transmission of data between different aspects of a system using the network. This is

No.	Time	Source	Destination	Protocol	Length	Info
311	11.376238	192.168.86.146	23.192.48.11	HTTP	594	GET /search?q=cybersecurity HTTP/1.1

Figure 1.1   Note that by default MIT uses HTTPS.

critically important to the overall security of the web app, because an attacker (or a curious user of your application) has several points at which they can insert themselves to inspect the traffic flowing between the front-end and various back-end pieces. If any of those insertion points contain data that is not encrypted (known as *plaintext*), the eavesdropper would at least be able to read the data and possibly be able to change the data to support their goals. Figure 1.1 shows what plaintext submission of a web search for "cybersecurity" looks like using http://web.mit.edu when viewed with the popular network analysis tool Wireshark. Note that every aspect of the communication is completely visible to the attacker. If credentials were being provided instead of a search term, such a disclosure could be disastrous.

As we start our exploration of data confidentiality, we'll first discuss some of the most common technical layouts for web applications. This will allow us to compare and contrast the advantages and disadvantages associated with each model.

Common Technical Layouts for Modern Web App Infrastructure

1. Fully cloud-based (serverless plus cloud storage)
   A fully cloud-based model – known commonly as a serverless model – is one where all of your web app's infrastructure is completely outsourced to a cloud provider's systems. You will have absolutely no physical hardware to manage, which can be a wonderful solution for developers with little space or resources. Moreover, as your web app's usage fluctuates, the resources allocated can scale up or down accordingly. Combined, these advantages lead to a reduction in bottom-line costs. Finally, leveraging the infrastructure of a highly reputable cloud provider can make some aspects of security (such as encryption of customer data in flight and at rest) easier.

   Conversely, a serverless approach does require additional considerations. Since your web app is no longer running on physical infrastructure that you connect to (or that is not within your enterprise perimeter), poorly configured access controls for your cloud app could lead to easier compromise from anywhere in the world. Moreover, if credentials are reused, modified in an easily identified way, or accidentally leaked (such as in a code commit), a single point of failure is introduced for additional cloud

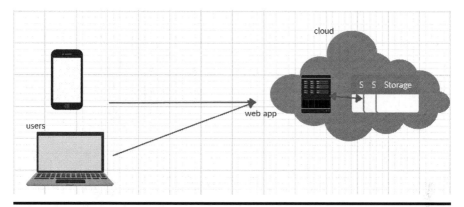

Figure 1.2   An example of a Cloud Server.

resources. Also, if the configuration of cloud resources is not well understood, there is significant risk in misconfiguring access to customer or internal data. And finally, if a cloud provider itself were compromised, your (and others') web apps could potentially be compromised much more systematically (Figure 1.2).

2. Hybrid (cloud front end with company [data center] storage, etc.)

A hybrid approach takes the best of both worlds available today. You'll have the front-end flexibility of scaling up and down dynamically based on the load to your web app, but you'll also have your critical data assets stored within your trusted enterprise (or similar) perimeter. Most of the front-end attacks – those compromising your web app or the cloud infrastructure itself – will remain serious considerations, of course.

There are new risks associated with a hybrid mode, however. The first is that a compromise of your web app could potentially lead to a privileged route into your enterprise perimeter. Considering third-party compromises are a major problem for enterprises today, this should be carefully and regularly audited. The second new risk is that data in transit is now subject to passive and/or active analysis. Therefore, it is of the utmost importance that this data in transit be encrypted with a probabilistic algorithm using strong keys (Figure 1.3).

3. Fully on-premise

A fully on-premise web app is the traditional model historically used. This requires a developer to set up physical or virtual servers to handle both the front-end and back-end aspects of the web app, which means that scaling up and down (unless you have an extremely robust infrastructure) will be severely limited. This will lead to additional costs in terms of space, time, and complexity.

Because everything is on-premise, this layout is able to leverage the trust and security built into your perimeter (such as access control), which should

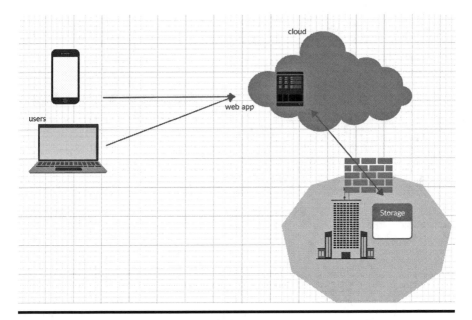

Figure 1.3 A Combination of On Premises and Cloud Server Infrastructures.

simplify the administrative security of your web app. However, a compromise of the web app may lead to privileged access to your internal infrastructure. Additionally, managing your own infrastructure for the web app will require that you get and manage your own certificates instead of relying on those served by the cloud provider. (Figure 1.4)

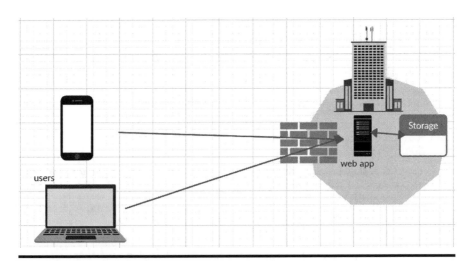

Figure 1.4 A 100% On Premises Server Model.

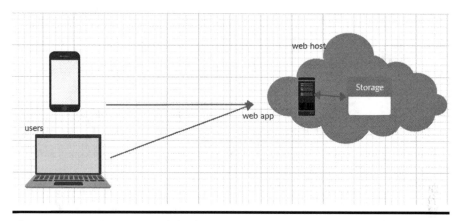

Figure 1.5 A Server Model That Is Outsourced To An Internet Service Provider (ISP).

4. Third-party managed (web hosting, etc.)

Using a third-party hosting provider for your web app is also possible. In doing so, you're effectively paying for the cost of an on-premise solution, but without the need for physical space, but also without the flexibility of a serverless cloud infrastructure. Depending on the hosting provider and package provided, the capabilities can be relatively basic (and cheap) or complex (and usually more expensive).

In terms of pros and cons, you're getting some of the cost- and space-based advantages of a cloud-based deployment, but with most of their disadvantages. You'll likely need to provide your own certificates as well (Figure 1.5).

Encrypting Data in Flight

Of course, deciding on an infrastructure for your web application is only half the battle of data confidentiality. The other half – taking precautions to keep clients' data secure in flight – is crucial for the success of your web app.

When a user visits your web app, they will expect that the data they are sending to it is taking its journey via strong encryption. Moreover, it is important that a well-established and trusted protocol is used to encrypt the data. In virtually all cases, the TLS protocol is used to perform this step.

TLS

TLS is a protocol built on top of TCP that provides the ability to perform a "handshake" between the client (your end user) and the server (wherever your web app is hosted) that establishes a secure connection using encryption. The specifics – such as which cipher suite will be used to generate a strong symmetric key for the session being set up – are negotiated during the steps of the handshake.

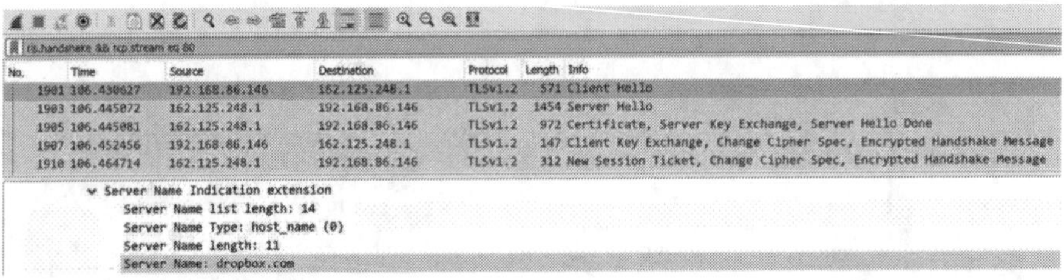

Figure 1.6

Figure 1.6 shows an example of a TLS v1.2 handshake with dropbox.com.

The first message in the handshake is a *Client Hello*, which essentially is the client's way of beginning the TLS negotiation with your web app. While there are quite a large number of pieces of information sent in this message, take note of just a couple.

1. Cipher Suites:

    The cipher suites in a TLS *Client Hello* message are the encryption algorithms that the client is willing to support when setting up a secure session with the server supporting your web app.

    The possible list of values is specified by RFCs defining different versions of TLS itself. In this case (Figure 1.7), the list of cipher suites is associated with TLSv1.2.[1] The values themselves refer to:

    - The protocol (TLS)
    - Which encryption algorithm is used (such as AES)
    - The length of the key (often 128 or 256 bits)
    - Which kind of encryption method is used (such as CBC)
    - The hashing algorithm leveraged (such as SHA256)

    When your server responds to this message in the *Server Hello* (Figure 1.8), it will choose one of the cipher suites listed earlier to be used for creating the key.

    Although explaining the details of each of the terms associated with the cipher suites is beyond the scope of this book, the best practice is to leverage the strongest cipher suite the client offers that supports the level of security you need. In the case of the session we're exploring here, we see that dropbox. com has selected *TLS_ECDHE_RSA_WITH_AES_128_GCM_SHA256*. This is the fifth-most preferred cipher suite by the client, since cipher suites in the *Client Hello* are ordered in descending order of preference. However, since this cipher suite for this version of TLS is preferred by the server over the others, it is selected.

2. Server Name Indication:

    The Server Name Indication (SNI) field of the *Client Hello* is the field that identifies the exact domain or subdomain that the client is visiting. This

```
tls.handshake && tcp.stream eq 80
```

No.	Time	Source	Destination	Protocol	Length	Info
1901	106.430627	192.168.86.146	162.125.248.1	TLSv1.2	571	Client Hello
1903	106.445072	162.125.248.1	192.168.86.146	TLSv1.2	1454	Server Hello
1905	106.445081	162.125.248.1	192.168.86.146	TLSv1.2	972	Certificate,
1907	106.452456	192.168.86.146	162.125.248.1	TLSv1.2	147	Client Key Ex
1910	106.464714	162.125.248.1	192.168.86.146	TLSv1.2	312	New Session 1

```
  ∨ Cipher Suites (17 suites)
        Cipher Suite: Reserved (GREASE) (0x9a9a)
        Cipher Suite: TLS_AES_128_GCM_SHA256 (0x1301)
        Cipher Suite: TLS_AES_256_GCM_SHA384 (0x1302)
        Cipher Suite: TLS_CHACHA20_POLY1305_SHA256 (0x1303)
        Cipher Suite: TLS_ECDHE_ECDSA_WITH_AES_128_GCM_SHA256 (0xc02b)
        Cipher Suite: TLS_ECDHE_RSA_WITH_AES_128_GCM_SHA256 (0xc02f)
        Cipher Suite: TLS_ECDHE_ECDSA_WITH_AES_256_GCM_SHA384 (0xc02c)
        Cipher Suite: TLS_ECDHE_RSA_WITH_AES_256_GCM_SHA384 (0xc030)
        Cipher Suite: TLS_ECDHE_ECDSA_WITH_CHACHA20_POLY1305_SHA256 (0xcca9)
        Cipher Suite: TLS_ECDHE_RSA_WITH_CHACHA20_POLY1305_SHA256 (0xcca8)
        Cipher Suite: TLS_ECDHE_RSA_WITH_AES_128_CBC_SHA (0xc013)
        Cipher Suite: TLS_ECDHE_RSA_WITH_AES_256_CBC_SHA (0xc014)
        Cipher Suite: TLS_RSA_WITH_AES_128_GCM_SHA256 (0x009c)
        Cipher Suite: TLS_RSA_WITH_AES_256_GCM_SHA384 (0x009d)
        Cipher Suite: TLS_RSA_WITH_AES_128_CBC_SHA (0x002f)
        Cipher Suite: TLS_RSA_WITH_AES_256_CBC_SHA (0x0035)
        Cipher Suite: TLS_RSA_WITH_3DES_EDE_CBC_SHA (0x000a)
```

Figure 1.7

```
tls.handshake && tcp.stream eq 80
```

No.	Time	Source	Destination	Protocol	Length	Info
1901	106.430627	192.168.86.146	162.125.248.1	TLSv1.2	571	Client Hello
1903	106.445072	162.125.248.1	192.168.86.146	TLSv1.2	1454	Server Hello
1905	106.445081	162.125.248.1	192.168.86.146	TLSv1.2	972	Certificate, Server Key Exchang
1907	106.452456	192.168.86.146	162.125.248.1	TLSv1.2	147	Client Key Exchange, Change Cip
1910	106.464714	162.125.248.1	192.168.86.146	TLSv1.2	312	New Session Ticket, Change Ciph

```
∨ Transport Layer Security
  ∨ TLSv1.2 Record Layer: Handshake Protocol: Server Hello
        Content Type: Handshake (22)
        Version: TLS 1.2 (0x0303)
        Length: 76
     ∨ Handshake Protocol: Server Hello
           Handshake Type: Server Hello (2)
           Length: 72
           Version: TLS 1.2 (0x0303)
         > Random: 5d54b6e0cdc1e0b05120054670d3a2faec13316957909f0a…
           Session ID Length: 0
           Cipher Suite: TLS_ECDHE_RSA_WITH_AES_128_GCM_SHA256 (0xc02f)
```

Figure 1.8

Figure 1.9

would typically be the name of the page where your web app is accessible. In this case, we see that we're visiting dropbox.com (Figure 1.9), which matches the name of the site where the Dropbox web app is hosted and the name on its certificate (Figure 1.10; more on that later).

Certificate

The next message in the handshake (Figure 1.11) carries the server's certificate. This information is used to attest that the site being connected to is in fact the same as the site we requested.

Figure 1.10

No.	Time	Source	Destination	Protocol	Length	Info
1903	106.445072	162.125.248.1	192.168.86.146	TLSv1.2	1454	Server Hello
1905	106.445081	162.125.248.1	192.168.86.146	TLSv1.2	972	Certificate, Server Key Exchange, !
1907	106.452456	192.168.86.146	162.125.248.1	TLSv1.2	147	Client Key Exchange, Change Cipher
1910	106.464714	162.125.248.1	192.168.86.146	TLSv1.2	312	New Session Ticket, Change Cipher !

```
    v Certificate: 3082082b30820713a003020102021005397e6ddd4ae63d74… (id-at-commonName=www.dropbox.com,id-
        v signedCertificate
            version: v3 (2)
            serialNumber: 0x05397e6ddd4ae63d74909da138a71e0c
          > signature (sha256WithRSAEncryption)
          v issuer: rdnSequence (0)
              v rdnSequence: 4 items (id-at-commonName=DigiCert SHA2 Extended Validation Server CA,id-at-or;
                > RDNSequence item: 1 item (id-at-countryName=US)
                > RDNSequence item: 1 item (id-at-organizationName=DigiCert Inc)
                > RDNSequence item: 1 item (id-at-organizationalUnitName=www.digicert.com)
                > RDNSequence item: 1 item (id-at-commonName=DigiCert SHA2 Extended Validation Server CA)
          v validity
              v notBefore: utcTime (0)
                  utcTime: 17-11-14 00:00:00 (UTC)
              v notAfter: utcTime (0)
                  utcTime: 20-02-11 12:00:00 (UTC)
          v subject: rdnSequence (0)
              v rdnSequence: 9 items (id-at-commonName=www.dropbox.com,id-at-organizationName=Dropbox, Inc,
                > RDNSequence item: 1 item (id-at-businessCategory=Private Organization)
                > RDNSequence item: 1 item (jurisdictionOfIncorporationCountryName=US)
                > RDNSequence item: 1 item (jurisdictionOfIncorporationStateOrProvinceName=Delaware)
                > RDNSequence item: 1 item (id-at-serialNumber=4348296)
                > RDNSequence item: 1 item (id-at-countryName=US)
                > RDNSequence item: 1 item (id-at-stateOrProvinceName=California)
                > RDNSequence item: 1 item (id-at-localityName=San Francisco)
                > RDNSequence item: 1 item (id-at-organizationName=Dropbox, Inc)
                > RDNSequence item: 1 item (id-at-commonName=www.dropbox.com)
```

Figure 1.11

The server's certificate will provide information about the issuer of the certificate, which includes:

- Country name (here, US)
- Organization (DigiCert, Inc., a trusted certificate authority)
- Organizational unit
- Common name

Because Dropbox is the subject of this certificate, we'll see similar information identifying both it and the website. Moreover, this certificate is only valid for a certain period of time (in this case, a little more than two years), which means that a new certificate will need to be requested before the end date.

We'll talk more about certificates in the next section, but for now know that using a trusted certificate authority like DigiCert is a requirement for deploying a web app that you wish people to trust.

Setting Up the Session

The next set of messages that are exchanged between the client and server are *Server Key Exchange* and *Client Key Exchange*. In these messages, the agreed-upon cipher suite is used to generate cryptographic information that will be used in creating the session key. Because this step varies based on the selected algorithm and delves deep into cryptographic principles, it is beyond the scope of this book.

```
∨ Transport Layer Security
    ∨ TLSv1.2 Record Layer: Handshake Protocol: Server Key Exchange
        Content Type: Handshake (22)
        Version: TLS 1.2 (0x0303)
        Length: 300
    ∨ Handshake Protocol: Server Key Exchange
        Handshake Type: Server Key Exchange (12)
        Length: 296
      ∨ EC Diffie-Hellman Server Params
            Curve Type: named_curve (0x03)
            Named Curve: x25519 (0x001d)
            Pubkey Length: 32
            Pubkey: e046a09dfe5e33e1c9a0068e68d11f14a0aafd833b98cfed…
          > Signature Algorithm: rsa_pss_rsae_sha256 (0x0804)
            Signature Length: 256
            Signature: aa88d948e512c35b027a2b1ea96b747c0dc8c6dbbf061578…
```

No.	Time	Source	Destination	Protocol	Length	Info
1903	106.445072	162.125.248.1	192.168.86.146	TLSv1.2	1454	Server Hello
1905	106.445081	162.125.248.1	192.168.86.146	TLSv1.2	972	Certificate, Server
1907	106.452456	192.168.86.146	162.125.248.1	TLSv1.2	147	Client Key Exchange,
1910	106.464714	162.125.248.1	192.168.86.146	TLSv1.2	312	New Session Ticket,

```
> Frame 1907: 147 bytes on wire (1176 bits), 147 bytes captured (1176 bits) on interface 0
> Ethernet II, Src: Microsof_64:df:a6 (28:16:a8:64:df:a6), Dst: Tp-LinkT_a9:4a:b1 (f4:f2:6d:a9:4a:
> Internet Protocol Version 4, Src: 192.168.86.146, Dst: 162.125.248.1
> Transmission Control Protocol, Src Port: 52913, Dst Port: 443, Seq: 518, Ack: 3719, Len: 93
∨ Transport Layer Security
  ∨ TLSv1.2 Record Layer: Handshake Protocol: Client Key Exchange
        Content Type: Handshake (22)
        Version: TLS 1.2 (0x0303)
        Length: 37
      ∨ Handshake Protocol: Client Key Exchange
            Handshake Type: Client Key Exchange (16)
            Length: 33
          ∨ EC Diffie-Hellman Client Params
                Pubkey Length: 32
                Pubkey: 2852176360f6e7f489cedda17682fc8343a2e31b43b5e952…
```

Finishing the Handshake

Now that each side has generated and shared the appropriate cryptographic information with the other side, all that's left to do is set up the session key and switch over to encrypted communications. This is accomplished with the *New Session Ticket* and *Change Cipher Spec* messages.

```
tls.handshake && tcp.stream eq 80
```

No.	Time	Source	Destination	Protocol	Length	Info
1903	106.445072	162.125.248.1	192.168.86.146	TLSv1.2	1454	Server Hello
1905	106.445081	162.125.248.1	192.168.86.146	TLSv1.2	972	Certificate, Serve
1907	106.452456	192.168.86.146	162.125.248.1	TLSv1.2	147	Client Key Exchang
1910	106.464714	162.125.248.1	192.168.86.146	TLSv1.2	312	New Session Ticket

```
> Internet Protocol Version 4, Src: 162.125.248.1, Dst: 192.168.86.146
> Transmission Control Protocol, Src Port: 443, Dst Port: 52913, Seq: 3719, Ack: 1006, Len: 258
∨ Transport Layer Security
  ∨ TLSv1.2 Record Layer: Handshake Protocol: New Session Ticket
      Content Type: Handshake (22)
      Version: TLS 1.2 (0x0303)
      Length: 202
    ∨ Handshake Protocol: New Session Ticket
        Handshake Type: New Session Ticket (4)
        Length: 198
      ∨ TLS Session Ticket
          Session Ticket Lifetime Hint: 86400 seconds (1 day)
          Session Ticket Length: 192
          Session Ticket: a75ab8ec2cd25b95ae408b47b1c69259ac17d7ddc8f443ee…
```

Figure 1.12

Figure 1.12 is the capture of the parameters (cipher suite plus the culmination of the key exchange steps) that can be used to validate the client and communicate with it for as long as the ticket is valid and the client provides it.

The final messages – *Change Cipher Spec* – are sent by both client and server and are intended to alert the other side that the rest of the communications will be encrypted using the session key mutually identified earlier.

For more in-depth resources regarding TLS and encrypted communications, we recommend reading *Bulletproof SSL and TLS: Understanding and Deploying SSL/TLS and PKI to Secure Servers and Web Applications* by Ivan Ristić.[2]

Site Validity

Now that we know how to set up the web app's infrastructure and ensure that the data in flight is encrypted, it's time to talk about site validity – helping the user to trust that they are using the right web app.

Proving Your Web App Is What It Says It Is

The first step in this process involves deploying a certificate that has been issued by a trusted certificate authority (CA). This means that the server is attesting to the client that the site where the web app is hosted is in fact associated with the certificate being served. If for some reason the site hosting the app is not associated with the site, an error will be shown.

Your connection is not private

Attackers might be trying to steal your information from **wrong.host.badssl.com** (for example, passwords, messages, or credit cards). Learn more

NET::ERR_CERT_COMMON_NAME_INVALID

☐ Help improve Safe Browsing by sending some system information and page content to Google. Privacy policy

Hide advanced   Back to safety

This server could not prove that it is **wrong.host.badssl.com**; its security certificate is from ***.badssl.com**. This may be caused by a misconfiguration or an attacker intercepting your connection.

Proceed to wrong.host.badssl.com (unsafe)

Figure 1.13

Commonly, errors can indicate that there is a third party intercepting and/or trying to manipulate the data (a man in the middle attack; see Figure 1.13), that the site owner has forgotten to renew their certificate (Figure 1.14), that some aspect of the certificate was deemed to no longer be trustworthy (Figure 1.15), or that the strength of the certificate isn't good enough per the requirements set out by the client (Figure 1.16).

Yet even if there is not an error, that doesn't mean that the certificate should be trusted in all cases. The term certificate authority is intended to refer to a relatively small number of organizations where trust for the majority of Internet sites (and therefore web apps) is granted. These CAs have an incentive to carefully control the certificates they create because a mis-certification can, at the least, cause negative publicity[3] and, at the worst, destroy their business.[4] Additionally, there are many cases where developers (especially during initial testing) will use self-signed certificates. In these cases, the trust of the underlying site and web app is only conferred by the local system (whether that is an internal server or a hosting provider). Because these organizations (i.e., the developer or the hosting provider) are not explicitly focused on safeguarding these certificates, issues – such as the inability to revoke a compromised certificate, or the ease of impersonating a site – abound. In fact, most common browsers *will* actually produce an error (Figure 1.17).

Your connection is not private

Attackers might be trying to steal your information from **expired.badssl.com** (for example, passwords, messages, or credit cards). Learn more

NET::ERR_CERT_DATE_INVALID

☐ Help improve Safe Browsing by sending some system information and page content to Google. Privacy policy

Hide advanced   Back to safety

This server could not prove that it is **expired.badssl.com**; its security certificate expired 1,583 days ago. This may be caused by a misconfiguration or an attacker intercepting your connection. Your computer's clock is currently set to Sunday, August 11, 2019. Does that look right? If not, you should correct your system's clock and then refresh this page.

Proceed to expired.badssl.com (unsafe)

Figure 1.14

Testing Your Web App's Confidentiality and Trust

Once you've set up your web app with a certificate and TLS, it is a great idea to test it across a wide variety of use cases to make sure that you've not missed anything. A wonderful resource is the Qualys SSL Labs' SSL Server Test.[5]

What Kind of Trust?

In addition to simply being able to get a certificate for your web app, there are actually different levels of trust afforded by different types of certificates. The most common is a standard, single-domain certificate. Most of the Internet uses this kind of certificate, as it provides certification similar to that of the example we explored in the previous section.

In fact, in the past few years, the push for encryption across the Internet has been so strong that at least one major company has emerged that will issue certificates for your site *free of charge*. This company, called Let's Encrypt, has helped to usher in the encryption of nearly every site (Figure 1.18).

Your connection is not private

Attackers might be trying to steal your information from **revoked.badssl.com** (for example, passwords, messages, or credit cards). Learn more

NET::ERR_CERT_REVOKED

☐ Help improve Safe Browsing by sending some system information and page content to Google. Privacy policy

<table>
<tr><td>Hide advanced</td><td>Reload</td></tr>
</table>

revoked.badssl.com normally uses encryption to protect your information. When Google Chrome tried to connect to revoked.badssl.com this time, the website sent back unusual and incorrect credentials. This may happen when an attacker is trying to pretend to be revoked.badssl.com, or a Wi-Fi sign-in screen has interrupted the connection. Your information is still secure because Google Chrome stopped the connection before any data was exchanged.

You cannot visit revoked.badssl.com right now because its certificate has been revoked. Network errors and attacks are usually temporary, so this page will probably work later.

Figure 1.15

Unfortunately, with that comes confusion for the average user. While certificates for most of the history of the Internet conferred some additional level of trust (on average), this is no longer the case.

Another option is to leverage an Extended Validation (EV) certificate, which actually requires manual steps to guarantee that an entity[7]:

■ Legally and physically exists
■ Has the proper authorization to have the certificate issued
■ Is authorized to use the domain they're trying to certify
■ Actually matches records associated with its alleged identity

These certificates are *much* harder to fake, but they are also much less rarely used and are more expensive than standard certificates.

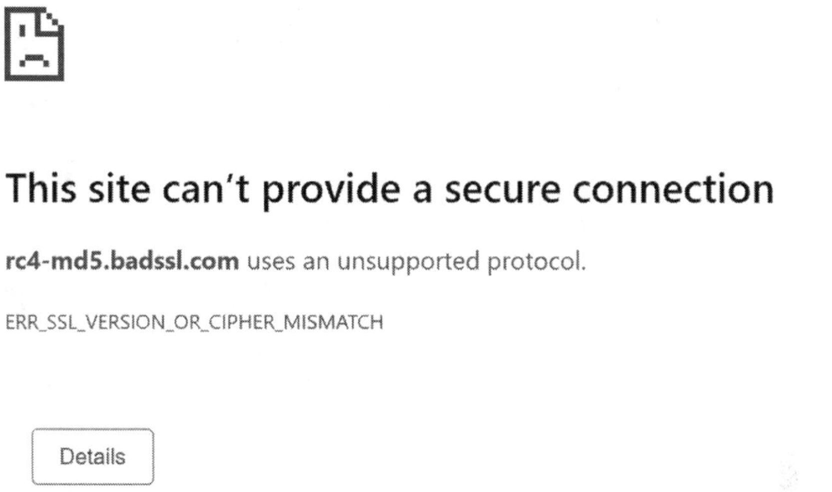

This site can't provide a secure connection

rc4-md5.badssl.com uses an unsupported protocol.

ERR_SSL_VERSION_OR_CIPHER_MISMATCH

Details

Figure 1.16

Spoofing and Related Concerns

Earlier we discussed certificates and how they can be used to identify that a site is what it says it is. But there's more to the story than simply trusting a site that seems to be correct and accurate (Figure 1.19). It is extraordinarily easy for attackers to

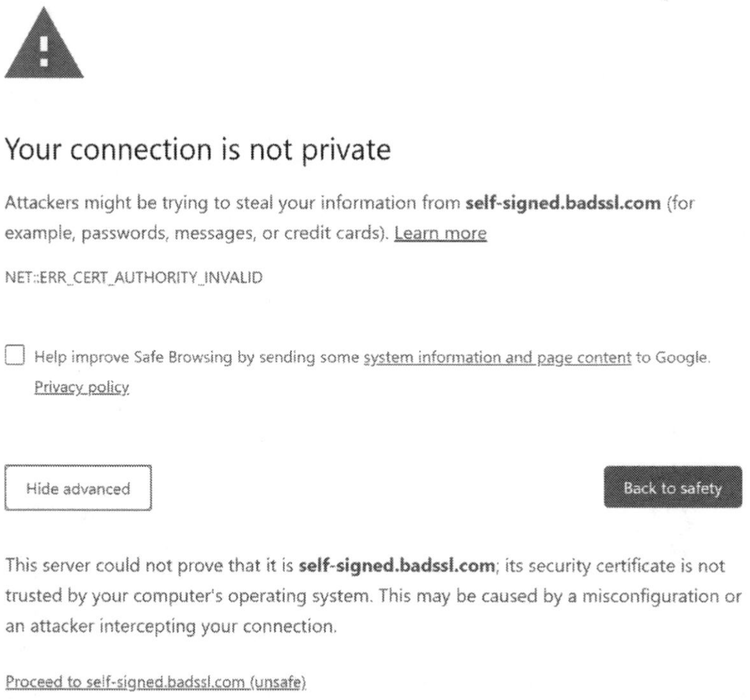

Your connection is not private

Attackers might be trying to steal your information from **self-signed.badssl.com** (for example, passwords, messages, or credit cards). Learn more

NET::ERR_CERT_AUTHORITY_INVALID

☐ Help improve Safe Browsing by sending some system information and page content to Google. Privacy policy

Hide advanced   Back to safety

This server could not prove that it is **self-signed.badssl.com**; its security certificate is not trusted by your computer's operating system. This may be caused by a misconfiguration or an attacker intercepting your connection.

Proceed to self-signed.badssl.com (unsafe)

Figure 1.17

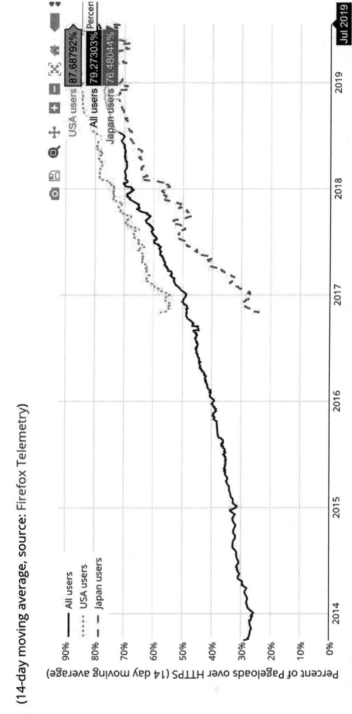

Figure 1.18   Let's Encrypt statistics.[6]

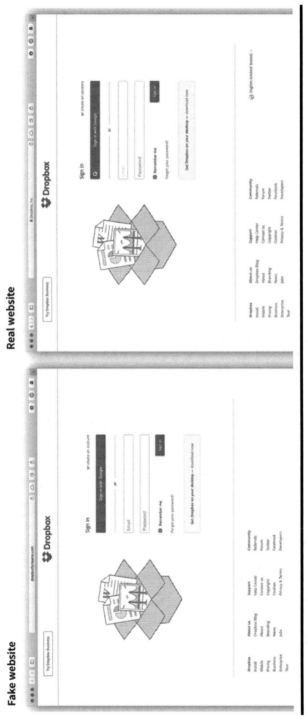

Figure 1.19

clone your site to look and behave identically like the real thing (at least superficially). The *Medium* blog post[8] from 2017 by Sebastian Conijn discusses in detail how he pretended to be Dropbox to compromise his colleague.

In addition, because the number of top-level domains that can be registered for a given domain has exploded in recent years, it is extremely easy to register a look-alike domain name (like *yourwebapp.info*) that you may not have thought to reserve.

Conclusion

In this section, we discussed web app security from the lens of network security. In doing so, we discussed two major topics: data confidentiality and site validity. In the former, we talked in detail about the importance of encrypting data in flight and how different physical and virtual layouts can leave vantage points for different kinds of attackers. In the latter section, we discussed the importance of using certificates to confer trust to the users of your web app. We also explored the topic of extended validation certificates for stronger levels of trust and how standard certificates – combined with clever attackers – can easily imitate your web app.

Resources

https://www.livescience.com/20727-internet-history.html
https://blog.secureideas.com/2018/04/a-brief-evolution-of-web-apps.html
https://www.digitalinformationworld.com/2018/11/infographic-the-short-history-of-website-building.html
https://intetics.com/blog/a-brief-history-of-software-development-methodologies
https://www.sas.com/en_us/insights/analytics/what-is-artificial-intelligence.html
https://www.sas.com/en_us/insights/analytics/machine-learning.html
https://searchnetworking.techtarget.com/definition/virtual-private-network
https://www.beyondtrust.com/blog/entry/difference-between-a-threat-actor-hacker-attacker
https://www.owasp.org/index.php/Cross-site_Scripting_(XSS)
Easttom, Chuck. Network Defense and Countermeasures, 3rd Edition. Published by Pearson Education, Inc.

References

1. https://www.ietf.org/rfc/rfc5246.txt
2. https://www.feistyduck.com/books/bulletproof-ssl-and-tls/
3. https://www.esecurityplanet.com/browser-security/google-hit-again-by-unauthorized-ssltls-certificates.html
4. https://www.wired.com/2011/09/diginotar-bankruptcy/
5. https://www.ssllabs.com/ssltest/index.html
6. https://letsencrypt.org/stats/
7. https://www.digicert.com/ev-ssl-certification/
8. https://medium.com/hike-one-digital-product-design/how-i-used-phishing-to-get-my-colleagues-passwords-this-is-how-i-did-it-73b9215689f1

Chapter 2

Cryptography

When one thinks of a web application, very often it is the front end that is conjured up. When we talk about this "front end," it is very often the first part that you see in a website after typing in the domain or the uniform resource locator (URL). Likewise, the front end can also be the shopping site of an online merchant, from whom you can purchase various goods and products. But as we eluded to in Chapter 1, today, much more is involved with a web application than just managing the front end.

For example, there is the back end, which is the database. From here, all sorts of information and data are stored, such as the personal identifiable information (PII) of customers, all of the transactions that occur from the device of the end user to the web application (and vice versa), and all of the mission-critical files that are needed to run the web application in an efficient and seamless fashion.

The other consideration in a web application is the security perspective. Given the rapidly changing cyberthreat landscape of today and just how prevalent, covert, and stealthy cyberattacks have become, securing all angles of the web application must be one of the highest priorities for a business or a corporation.

For example, the lines of network communications that are used to communicate back and forth between the device of the end user to the web application must be made as secure as possible, and in fact, invisible to the outside world. This is so that any confidential information and data cannot be easily intercepted by a malicious third party, such as that of a cyberattacker.

This is what was reviewed in great length in Chapter 1 of this book, which was all about the network security issues that a web application and the server that it resides upon faces. In particular, the following topics were examined in great detail:

- A chronological history of the Internet
- The evolution of web applications
- the fundamentals of network security – The OSI model
- Assessing a threat to a web application.
- Network security terminology
- The types of network security topologies best suited for web applications
- The types of attacks that can take place against web applications
- How to protect web applications from DDoS attacks
- Defending web applications at a deeper level
- How to properly implement a firewall to safeguard the web application
- The use of intrusion detection systems
- The use of virtual private networks (VPNs) to protect a web application server
- How to assess the current state of security of a web application server
- How to conduct the initial security assessment on the web application
- Techniques used by the cyberattacker against the web application and the web application server

In this chapter of the book, we focus exclusively on how the confidential information that is transmitted back and forth between the device of the end user and the web application (and vice versa) can be scrambled into a garbled state so that even if this were to be intercepted by a cyberattacker, it would be rendered completely useless, unless he or she had the actual keys to unscramble it. This is specifically known as encryption. It is also just as equally important, if not more so, to have the same levels of encryption in the web application server.

The science of encryption and decryption (which is essentially the rendering of the garbled state of the information and data into a comprehensible and understandable state) is known as cryptography, which is the focal point of this chapter. Specifically, this chapter will cover the following.

An Introduction to Cryptography

Cryptography is a science that dates all the way back to the times of Julius Caesar. In its simplest terms, the science of cryptography is merely the scrambling and the descrambling of text, or written messages, between two individual parties. These individual parties can also be referred to as the sender and the receiver. The sender creates the text or the written message that needs to be sent, and the receiver (as the name implies) receives the text or the written message and then reads it and appropriately responds.

In normal, everyday communications, we always trust that the individual party who is receiving the message will do so without any type of problem. While this does mostly happen in our daily lives, given especially the high-tech world we live in today, this sometimes does not occur.

And when the message is not received, we always assume that the worst has occurred. But what is the worst that could happen? Well, the message could be intercepted by a third party and maliciously used. Now once again, in normal everyday conversations, while we would normally trust the receiving party to keep the details of the conversation secret, there is always a chance that a third party could be covertly listening in and use that privileged information for purposes of personal gain or exploitation, such as that of identity theft.

We can also extend this example to electronic communications of all types. For example, when we hit the "send" button, what assurances do we have that the receiving party will get our message or that it will not be intercepted by a third party? Obviously, we cannot really ensure any type of safety, especially when it comes to electronic communications, which are transmitted all over worldwide networks and the Internet.

The only thing that can be guaranteed is that if any type of message were to be captured by a third party, it would be rendered useless. But how is this task actually accomplished? It is done by the scrambling and descrambling of the message. Specifically, the message is scrambled by the sending party, and it remains scrambled while it is in transit, until the receiving party gets the text or the written message.

Message Scrambling and Descrambling

At this point, the message must be unscrambled in order for it to make sense to the receiving party. For example, a very simple example of this is "I LOVE YOU." The sending party would scramble this message by rearranging the letters as "UYO I VEOL." This message would then stay in this scrambled format while it is in transit, until it is received by the other party. The receiving party would then descramble it, so it would read once again "I LOVE YOU." So, if this message were to have been captured by a third party, the content would be rendered useless and totally undecipherable to them. This, in very simple terms, is the science of cryptography.

Specifically, cryptography can be defined as "the practice and study of techniques for secure communication in the presence of third parties (called adversaries). More generally, it is about constructing and analyzing that overcome the influence of adversaries and which are related to the various aspects of data confidentiality, data integrity, authentication, and repudiation."[1]

Cryptography intersects with other branches of study, especially that of mathematics and computer sciences, and even biometrics, into the new field known as biocryptography. This will be examined in more detail, later in this chapter, after some of the more fundamental concepts have been covered.

Encryption and Decryption

In terms of cryptography, scrambling and descrambling are also known as encryption and decryption, respectively. So, for instance, the written message of "I LOVE YOU" when scrambled by the sending party becomes what is known as the "encrypted message," meaning that it has been disguised in such a manner that it would be totally meaningless, or in the terms of cryptography, it would be what is known as undecipherable.

Also, encryption can be further defined and described as the "conversion of information from a readable state to apparent nonsense."[1] Now, when the receiving party receives this encrypted written message, it must be descrambled into an understandable and comprehensible state of context. This process of descrambling is known as decryption.

So, rather than saying that cryptography is the science of scrambling and descrambling, it can now be referred to as the science of encryption and decryption. Specific terms are also used for the encrypted message and the decrypted message. For example, the decrypted message, when it is returned into its plain or original state of context, which is comprehensible and decipherable, is also known as cleartext or plaintext.

Ciphertexts

When the decrypted message is once again encrypted into a state of context that is totally incomprehensible and undecipherable, this is known as ciphertext. So, to illustrate all of this, with the previous example, when the sending party creates the written message of "I LOVE YOU," this is the plaintext or the cleartext.

Once this message is encrypted into the format of "UYO I VEOL," and while it is in transit, it becomes known as the ciphertext. Then, once the receiving party gets this ciphertext and then decrypts it into a comprehensible and understandable form of "I LOVE YOU," this message then becomes the plaintext or the cleartext once again.

At this point, the question that often gets asked is how does the sending party actually encrypt the message and how does the receiving party then actually decrypt the ciphertext? Well, in its simplest form, the written message is encrypted via a special mathematical formula. This formula is specifically known as the encryption algorithm. Because the ciphertext is now encrypted by this special mathematical algorithm, it would be rendered useless to a third party with malicious intent due to its totally garbled nature.

As the receiving party receives this ciphertext, it remains in its garbled format until is it is descrambled. To do this, a "key" is used, which is only known by the sending party and the receiving party. In terms of cryptography, this key is also known as the cipher, and it is usually a short string of characters, which is needed to break the ciphertext.

As will be examined later in this chapter, interestingly enough, the encryption algorithm is actually publicly known and is available for everyone to use. Therefore, the key or the ciphertext must remain a secret between the sending party and the receiving party.

In order to send the ciphertext between the sending party and the receiving party, as well to share the keys that are needed to encrypt and decrypt the ciphertext, specific cryptographic systems are needed. Today, two such types of systems exist. They are known as symmetric key systems and asymmetric key systems.

Symmetric Key Systems and Asymmetric Key Systems

The primary difference between these two types of cryptographic systems is that the former uses only one key for encryption and decryption, which is known as the private key of the ciphertext. With the latter, two types of keys are utilized for encryption and decryption of the ciphertext, and these are known as the public key and the private key.

We will look at both of these cryptographic systems, first starting with symmetric key systems. One of the simplest methodologies in symmetric key systems is that of the Caesar cipher, which can be attributed to as far back as Julius Caesar (thus its name).

The Caesar Methodology

With the Caesar methodology, each letter of the message is substituted with another letter of the alphabet, which is sequenced by so many spaces or letters later in the alphabet. To make things simpler to understand, we can denote this specific sequencing as "k". So, four letters out into the alphabet would be represented mathematically as $k = 4$.

Let us go back to our example once again of "I LOVE YOU." If $k = 4$, which represents the letter sequencing, the letter that would replace "I" in this plaintext message would be the letter "E." So, continuing in this fashion, the ciphertext would be translated as "E YOUA EIM." With the Caesar cipher, a technique known as "wrap-around" is possible. This means that once the last letter of the ciphertext is reached (which in this case would be the letter "Z"), it wraps around immediately to the start of the alphabet, with the letter "A."

So, if the wrap-around technique were needed to finish the encryption of this plaintext message, with $k = 4$, the letter "A" in the plaintext message would become the letter "D" and so on. The value of the "k" serves as the key in the Caesar cipher, since it specifies how the plaintext should be encrypted over into the ciphertext.

With the Caesar cipher, some 25 different combinations, or key values, can be used. An improvement over the Caesar cipher came with a newer technique known as the monoalphabetic cipher. What distinguishes this from the Caesar is that although one letter of the alphabet can still be replaced with another, no exact mathematical sequencing is required. Rather, the letters in the plaintext can be substituted at random in order to create the ciphertext. So once again, for example, the plaintext message of "I LOVE YOU" can be written at will and at random as "UYO VOLI E." With the monoalphabetic cipher, more pairings of letters are possible. For example, there are $10 \wedge 26$ possibilities of letter pairings versus only the 25 letter pairings available with the Caesar cipher.

Thus, if a hacker were to attempt a brute-force attack on a monoalphabetic cipher (which is just the sheer guessing of the ciphertext for any type of pattern in order to decipher the plaintext), it would obviously take a much longer time to crack versus the Caesar cipher.

Types of Cryptographic Attacks

With both of these types of cryptographic methods just described, there are three types of attacks they are vulnerable to, as follows:

1. Ciphertext-only attack: With this type of attack, only the ciphertext is known to the attacker. But if this particular individual is well trained in statistics, he or she can use various statistical techniques to convert the ciphertext back into the plaintext.
2. Known-plaintext attack: This occurs when the hacker knows some aspect of the letter pairings, thus, they can consequently convert the ciphertext back into the plaintext.
3. Chosen-plaintext attack: With this type of attack, the hacker can intercept the natural plaintext message that is being transmitted across the network medium, and from this, reverse-engineer it back into its ciphertext form in an attempt to figure out the specific encryption scheme.

Polyalphabetic Encryption

Over time, improvements were made to both the Caesar cipher and the monoalphabetic cipher. The next step up from these two techniques was another technique known as polyalphabetic encryption. With this, multiple types of Caesar ciphers are used, but these ciphers are used in a specific sequence, which repeats once the overall cipher has reached its logical end the first time, in order to finish the completion of the encryption of the plaintext message.

This means that the wrap-around technique is also prevalent in this type of scenario. Let us illustrate this example once again with "I LOVE YOU." Building upon the example used previously, suppose that two types of Caesar ciphers are being utilized, such as where k = 1, and k = 2 ("k" once again denotes the actual Caesar cipher, or the sequential spacing of the number of letters later in the alphabet).

The following chart demonstrates this in order to make it clearer:

Plaintext:	A B C D E F G H I J K L M N O P Q R S T U V W X Y Z
First Caesar Cipher, where k = 1	B C D E F G H I J K L M N O P Q R S T U V W X Y Z A
Second Caesar Cipher, where k = 2	C D E G H I J K L M N O P Q R S T U V W X Y Z A B C

The overall cipher algorithm utilized is C1 (k = 1), C2 (k = 2), where C denotes the Caesar key. So, with the example of using "I LOVE YOU," with the polyalphabetic algorithm, it would be encrypted as "J ORYF BPX." To understand this further, the first letter in the plaintext is C1, so I is represented as J, the second letter of the plaintext is C2, so C is represented as O, and so on.

The logical end of the cipher algorithm is C2, so once again, it reaches the logical end of its first iteration and then wraps around once again as C1 (k = 1), C2 (k = 2) the second time around, and then the third time around, until the plaintext message has been fully encrypted.

So, in our illustration of "I LOVE YOU," there were a total of three iterations of C1 (k = 1), C2 (k = 2), in order to fully encrypt the plaintext. Over the years, a more modern form of encryption was developed, known as the block cipher. With this method, the plaintext message is put together in one long stream, and from this, it is then broken up into blocks of text of equal value.

Block Ciphers

Using a method of transposition, the plaintext message is then encrypted into its scrambled format. Let us illustrate this again with our previous example, but this time, let us assume a block of three characters, mathematically represented as 3 bits, or where k = 3.

Plaintext:	I LOVE YOU
Plaintext Block:	ILO VEY OUX
Ciphertext Block:	OLI YEV XUO
Ciphertext:	OLIYEVXUO

Note that an extra character as added at the end, which is the letter "X." This was added so that a complete plaintext block can be formed. As a rule of thumb, if the total number of characters in the plaintext is not divisible by the block size permutation (in this instance, where k = 3), it can be safely assumed that extra characters will be needed in order for the last block of plaintext to be considered complete. This is known as padding. It should be noted that the most widely used block is where k = 8 bits long.

As we can see, even with the simple example provided earlier, block ciphers are a very powerful tool for symmetric key cryptographic systems. After all, it goes through a set number of iterations of scrambling in order to come up with a rather well-protected ciphertext. But despite these strong advantages of block ciphers, it does suffer from an inherent weakness, which if discovered by a hacker, can cause rather detrimental damage, with irrevocable results. This vulnerability is that two blocks can contain the exact same data. Let us examine this with our previous example once again. As it was illustrated, the ciphertext block was formulated as "OLI YEV XUO." But, of course, depending upon the actual written context of the plaintext, it is possible that the ciphertext block can contain two or more exact blocks of the same data.

Initialization Vectors

Continuing with our example, it would look like this: "OLI OLI YEV." To alleviate this weakness, a system of initialization vectors (IVs) is used. Although it sounds complex, simply put, this involves creating some further scrambling, or randomness, within the ciphertext block itself. However, it should be noted that it is not the IV itself that further encrypts the ciphertext blocks.

Cipher Block Chaining

Rather, the IVs are part of a much larger process known as cipher block chaining (CBC) for short. With this methodology, multiple loops of encryption are created in order to further scramble the ciphertext. Here is the how the process works:

1. The IV is created first.
2. Through a mathematical process known as XOR (which stands for eXclusive OR, and is used quite frequently to determine if the bits of two strings of data match or not), the first created IV is XOR'ed, with the first block of ciphertext data.
3. The first chunk of data that has been XOR'ed is further broken down by another layer of encryption.
4. This process is then continued until all of the blocks of ciphertext have been XOR'ed and enveloped with another layer of encryption.

Thus, this is how CBC got its name. For instance, steps 1–4 create the first loop or chain, the second loop or chain is then next initiated, and so on, until the ciphertext has been fully analyzed and encrypted by this methodology.

Disadvantages of Symmetric Key Cryptography

Now that we have reviewed some of the basic principles of symmetric key cryptography, although it can be a robust system to use, it does suffer from three major vulnerabilities, which are as follows:

1. Key distribution
2. Key storage and recovery
3. Open systems

With regard to the first one, key distribution, symmetric cryptography requires the sharing of secret keys between the two parties (sending and receiving), which requires the implicit trust that this key will not be shared with any other outside third party. The only way that any type of secrecy can be achieved in this regard would be to establish a secure channel.

While this works very well in theory, in practicality, it is not a feasible solution. For instance, the typical organization would not be able to afford implementing and deploying such a secure channel, except for the very large corporations and government entities. Thus, the only other solution available in this circumstance would be the use of a so-called designated "controller."

This third party would have to be very highly trusted by both the sending and the receiving parties. But this methodology of trust to create a secure channel can prove to be a very cumbersome task. For example, imagine a place of business. Suppose that the chief executive officer (CEO) decides to share the keys of the business with the employees who need access to it at irregular hours. Rather than trusting the employees explicitly, the CEO could decide to utilize a manager to whom the employees must give the key when they are done with their job duties, and from there, this same manager would then give this key to the next employee who needed access.

Already, one can see that this is a very tedious and time-consuming process, and to compound this problem even more, the designated controller, in this case the manager, cannot be trusted either because in between the distribution of keys to the employees, this manager could very well give these malicious keys to a malicious third party. As a result, this method does not guarantee the secrecy of the key that is needed to encrypt and decrypt the plaintext message.

In terms of key storage and capacity, let us take the example of a very large place organization, such as a multinational corporation. The problem of using the principles of symmetric cryptography becomes quite simple. First, since there will be many more lines of communication between the sending and the receiving parties, the need to implement that many more controllers becomes totally unrealistic as well as infeasible. Thus, the distribution of the keys can become a virtual nightmare.

Second, all of the private keys associated with symmetric cryptography have to be securely stored somewhere, primarily in a database that resides in a central server. As is well known, primary and central servers are often prone to worms, viruses, and other types of malicious software. Compounding this problem even more is the fact that the larger the number of private keys stored onto this central server, the greater the chances of the central server being hacked into.

A way that these private keys can be stolen is if a piece of malicious code is injected into the intranet of the corporate network, which in turn reaches the database. This malicious code then actually covertly hijacks these private keys and sends them back to the hacker.

Third, when companies and organizations become large, the chances that employees will require remote access to the corporate intranet and network resources become even greater. As a result, the private keys that are used to communicate between the sending and receiving parties can also be hijacked very quickly and easily by a hacker who has enough experience and knowledge.

Finally, with an open system, private or symmetric cryptography works best only when it is used in a very closed or "sterile" environment, where there are, at best, only just a few sending and receiving parties. But this is not the case with "open" or public environments, such as our example of the very large corporation. In these situations, there is simply no way to confirm the authenticity or the integrity of the private keys and their respective ciphertext messages.

So, as one can see, private keys and symmetric cryptography simply are inflexible, too costly, and do not scale well for most types of environments. For example, "solutions that are based on private-key cryptography are not sufficient to deal with the problem of secure communications in open systems where parties cannot physically meet, or where parties have transient interactions."[2]

Although there will never be a perfect 100% solution that will correct the flaws of symmetric cryptography, there is a partial solution known as the key distribution center (KDC), which is reviewed next.

The Key Distribution Center

The KDC is a central server that is dedicated solely to the KDC network configuration. It merely consists of a database of all of the end users in the organization and their respective passwords, as well other trusted servers and computers along the network.

It should be noted that these passwords are also encrypted. Now, if one end user wishes to communicate with another end user on a different computer system, the sending party enters their password into the KDC, using specialized software called Kerberos. When the password is received by the KDC, Kerberos then uses a special mathematical algorithm, which adds the receiving party's information and converts it over to a cryptographic key.

Once this encrypted key has been established, the KDC sets up and establishes other keys for the encryption of the communication session between the sending and the receiving party. These other keys are also referred to as the tickets. These tickets have a time expiration associated with them, so the ticket will expire at a predetermined point in time in order to prevent unauthorized use, and it would also be rendered useless if it is stolen, hijacked, or intercepted by a third party.

Although the KDC system does provide a partial solution to the shortcomings of symmetric key cryptography, the KDC also by nature has some major security flaws, such as:

1. Because the KDC contains all of the master keys and the access rules needed for encrypted communication, the server that contains the KDC system must be both logically and physically protected all the time. If an attack is successful on the KDC, the entire communications channel within the organization will completely break down. Also, personnel who have access to the KDC can easily decrypt the ciphertext messages between all of the sending and receiving parties.
2. The KDC process presents a single point of failure for the organization. If the server containing the KDC crashes, all kinds of secure communications become impossible, at least on a temporary basis. Also, since all of the end users will be hitting the KDC at peak times, the processing demands placed onto the KDC can be very great, thus heightening the chances that very slow communications between the sending and the receiving parties, or even a breakdown of the communications system, can also happen.

Mathematical Algorithms with Symmetric Cryptography

A number of key mathematical algorithms are associated with symmetric cryptography:

1. The Needham-Schroder algorithm: This algorithm was specifically designed for KDC systems in order to deal with sending and receiving parties from

within the organization who appear to be offline. For example, if the sending party sends a ciphertext message to the receiving party, and after sending the message they go offline, the KDC system could just literally "hang" and maintain an open session indefinitely until the sending party comes back online again. With this particular algorithm, this problem is averted by immediately terminating the communication session once either party goes offline.

2. The Digital Encryption Standard algorithm (DES): This mathematical algorithm was developed in 1975, and by 1981, it became the de facto algorithm for symmetric cryptography systems. This is a powerful algorithm, as it puts the ciphertext through 16 iterations in order to ensure full encryption.

3. The Triple Digit Encryption Standard algorithm (3DES): This mathematical algorithm was developed as an upgrade to the DES algorithm. The primary difference between the two of them is that 3DES puts the ciphertext through three times as many more iterations than the DES algorithm.

4. The International Data Encryption Algorithm (IDEA): This is a newer mathematical algorithm than 3DES and is constantly shifting the letters of the ciphertext message around until is decrypted by the receiving party. It is three times faster than any of the other DES algorithms just reviewed, and as a result, it does not consume as much processor power as the DES algorithms do.

5. The Advanced Encryption Standard algorithm (AES): This is the latest symmetric cryptography algorithm and was developed in 2000, primarily designed for use by the federal government.

The Hashing Function

Finally, in symmetric cryptography, it should be noted that all of the ciphertext messages come with what is known as a hash. It is a one-way mathematical function, meaning it can be encrypted, but it cannot be decrypted. Its primary purpose is not to encrypt the ciphertext; rather, its primary purpose is to prove that the message in the ciphertext has not changed in any way, shape, or form. This is also referred to as message integrity.

For example, if the sending party sends a message to the receiving party, the message (or the ciphertext) will have a hash function with it. The receiving party can then run a hash algorithm, and if the ciphertext message has remained intact, the receiving party can be assured that the message they have received is indeed authentic and has not been compromised in any way. But if the hash mathematical values are different, it is quite possible that the message is not authentic and that it has been compromised.

Earlier, we reviewed at length the principles of symmetric cryptography. With this methodology, only one key is used to encrypt and decrypt the ciphertext between the sending and the receiving parties. Now, in next section, we look at an entirely different methodology: asymmetric key cryptography. With this type of methodology, not just one key is used, but rather, two keys are used.

Asymmetric Key Cryptography

These keys are called the public and the private key, and are also used to encrypt and decrypt the ciphertext that is sent between the sending and the receiving parties as they communicate with another. In the simplest terms, asymmetric cryptography can be likened to that of a safe deposit box at a local bank. In this example, normally, two sets of keys are used. One key is one the bank gives you. This can be referred to as the public key, because it is used over and over again by past renters of this particular safety deposit box and for other, future renters as well. The second key is the private key, which the bank keeps in their possession at all times, and only the bank personnel know where it is kept.

The world of asymmetric cryptography is just like this example, but, of course, it is much more complex in practice. To start off with, typically, in asymmetric cryptography, it is the receiving party that is primarily responsible for generating both the public and the private key. In this situation, let us refer to the public key as "pk" and the private key as "sk." So, to represent both of these keys together, it would be mathematically represented as (pk, sk). It is then the sending party which uses the pk to encrypt the message they wish to send to the receiving party, which then uses the private key (sk) which they have privately and personally formulated to decrypt the encrypted ciphertext from the sending party.

Remember, one of the primary goals of asymmetric cryptography is to avoid the need for both the sending and the receiving parties from having to meet literally face to face in order to decide how to protect (or encrypt) their communications with another. So, at this point, the question that arises is: How does the sending party know about the pk generated by the receiving party so that the two can communicate with each other?

Public Keys and Public Private Keys

There are two distinct ways in which this can be accomplished: (1) The receiving party can deliberately and purposefully notify the sending party of the pk in a public channel, so that communications can be initiated and then further established; and (2) the sending party and the receiving party do not know anything about each other in advance. In this case, the receiving party makes their public key known on a global basis, so that whoever wishes to communicate with the receiving party can do so.

Now, this brings up a very important point: The public key is literally "public," meaning that anybody can use it, even all of the hackers in the world. So, how does asymmetric cryptography remain secure? It remains so based on the privacy of the private key (sk) which is being utilized. In these cases, it is then up to the receiving party now to share the private key (sk) with any other party, no matter how much they are trusted.

If the privacy of the sk is compromised in any way, then the security scheme of asymmetric cryptography is totally compromised. In order to help ensure that the private keys remain private, asymmetric cryptography uses the power of prime numbers. The basic idea here is to create a very large prime number as a product of multiplying two other very large prime numbers together.

Mathematically speaking, the basic premise is that it will take a hacker a very long time to figure out the two prime number multiples of a very large product, which is several hundred integers long, and thus, give up in frustration. Even if a hacker were to spend the time to figure out one of these prime numbers, the hacker still has to figure out the other prime number, and the chances that they will figure this out is almost nil.

As a result, only one portion of the (pk, sk) is figured out, and the asymmetric cryptography technique utilized by the sending and the receiving parties still remains intact and secure. In other words, the hacker cannot reverse-engineer one key to get the other key to break the ciphertext. It should also be noted than in asymmetric key cryptography, the same public key can be used by multiple, different sending parties to communicate with the single receiving party, thus forming a one-to-many, or 1:N, mathematical relationship.

The Differences Between Asymmetric and Symmetric Cryptography

Now that we have provided a starting point into asymmetric cryptography, it is important at this juncture to review some of the important distinctions and differences between this and symmetric cryptography. First, with symmetric cryptography, the complete 100% secrecy of the key must be assured, whereas asymmetric cryptography requires only half of the secret, namely that of the private key (sk).

Although this might seem like just a minor difference, the implications of this are great. For example, with symmetric cryptography, both the sender and the receiver need to be able to communicate the secret key generated with each other first, and the only way this can happen is if both parties met face to face with each other, before the encrypted communication can take place. And to complicate matters even more, it is absolutely imperative that this private or secret key is not shared with anybody else or even intercepted by a third party. But with asymmetric cryptography, the public key can be shared virtually indiscriminately, without the fear of compromising security.

Second, symmetric cryptography utilizes the same secret key for the encryption and decryption of the ciphertext, but with asymmetric cryptography, two different keys (namely the public and the private keys) are used for the encryption and the decryption of the ciphertext.

In other words, in asymmetric cryptography, the roles of the sender and the receiver are not interchangeable with one another, like with symmetric cryptography. This means that with asymmetric cryptography, the communication is only one way. As discussed, because of this, multiple senders can send their ciphertext to just one receiver, but in symmetric cryptography, only one sending party can communicate with just one receiving party.

Also, asymmetric cryptography possesses two key advantages: (1) It allows for the sending party(ies) and the receiving party to communicate with another, even if their lines of communication are being observed by a third party; and (2) because of the multiple-key nature, the receiving party needs to keep only one private key to communicate with the multiple sending parties.

The Disadvantages of Asymmetric Cryptography

But despite all of this, asymmetric cryptography does possess one very serious disadvantage: When compared to symmetric cryptography, it is two to three times much slower than symmetric cryptography. This is primarily because of the multiple parties and the multiple keys involved.

Thus, this takes enormous processing power and is a serious drain on server power and system resources. So far in our review of asymmetric cryptography, we have assumed that the potential hacker is merely just eavesdropping on the ciphertext communications between the sending and the receiving parties. But if the potential hacker has a strong criminal intent, they can quite easily listen in on the communications on an active basis and cause great harm in the end.

There are two specific cases in which this can happen. First is the situation where the hacker replaces a public key of his own (mathematically represented as pk') while the ciphertext is in transit between the sending and the receiving parties, and the receiving party decrypts that ciphertext with that malicious public key (pk'). But keep in mind, this scenario assumes that the hacker has some substantial information about the private key (sk).

The second situation arises when the hacker can change the mathematical value of the public key or change it while it is in transmission between the sending and the receiving parties. The exact techniques for protecting the public key in asymmetric cryptography will be discussed later in this chapter.

The Mathematical Algorithms of Asymmetric Cryptography

A number of key mathematical algorithms serve as the crux for asymmetric cryptography, and of course, use widely differing mathematical algorithms than the ones used with symmetric cryptography. The algorithms used in asymmetric cryptography are as follows:

1. The RSA algorithm
2. The Diffie-Hellman algorithm
3. The elliptical wave theory algorithm

In terms of the RSA Algorithm, this is probably the most famous and widely used asymmetric cryptography algorithm. In fact, this very algorithm will serve as the foundation for the discussion on biocryptography later in this chapter. The RSA algorithm originates from the RSA Data Security Corporation, and is named after the inventors who created it: Ron Rivest, Adi Shamir, and Leonard Adelman.

The RSA algorithm uses the power of prime numbers to create both the public key and the private key. But using such large keys to encrypt such large amounts of data is totally infeasible from the standpoint of processing power and central server resources. Instead, ironically, the encryption is done using symmetric algorithms (such as the ones reviewed previously), then the private key is further encrypted by the receiving party's public key.

Once the receiving party obtains their ciphertext from the sending party, the private key generated by the symmetric cryptography algorithm is decrypted, and then the public key that was generated by asymmetric cryptography can be subsequently used to decrypt the rest of the ciphertext.

In terms of the Diffie-Hellman asymmetric algorithm, it is named after its inventors as well: Whit Diffie and Martin Hellman. It is also known as the DH algorithm. But interestingly enough, this algorithm is not used for the encryption of the ciphertext; rather, the main concern is to address the problem of finding a solution of the issue of sending a key over a secure channel.

Here is a summary of how it works on a very simple level:

1. The receiving party, as usual, has the public key and the private key that they have generated, but this time, they both are created by the DH algorithm.
2. The sending party receives the public key generated by the receiving party and uses this DH algorithm to generate another set of public keys and private keys, but on a temporary basis.
3. The sending party now takes this newly created temporary private key and the public key sent by the receiving party to generate a random, secret number – this is known as the session key.

4. The sending party uses this newly established session key to encrypt the ciphertext message and sends this to the receiving party, with the public key that they have temporarily generated.
5. When the receiving party finally receives the ciphertext from the sending party, the session key can now be derived mathematically.
6. Once the previous step has been completed, the receiving party can now decrypt the rest of the ciphertext.

Finally, elliptical wave theory can be used to encrypt very large amounts of data, and its main advantage is that it is very quick and does not require a lot of server overhead or processing time. As its name implies, elliptical wave theory first starts with a parabolic curve drawn on a normal x,y coordinate Cartesian plane.

After the first series of X and Y coordinates are plotted, various lines are then drawn through the image of the curve, and this process continues until many more curves are created and their corresponding intersecting lines are also created.

Once this process has been completed, the plotted X and Y coordinates of each of the intersected lines and parabolic curves are then extracted. Once this extraction has been completed, all of the hundreds and hundreds of X and Y coordinates are then added together in order to create the public and the private keys. But the trick to decrypting a ciphertext message encrypted by elliptical wave theory is that the receiving party has to know the shape of the original elliptical curve and all of the X and Y coordinates of the lines where they intersect with the various curves, as well as the actual starting point at which the addition of the X and Y coordinates first started.

The Public Key Infrastructure

Since the public key has become so important in the encryption and the decryption of the ciphertext messages between the sending and receiving parties, and given the nature of its public role in the overall communication process, great pains and extensive research have been undertaken to create an infrastructure that would make the process of creating and sending the public keys, as well as the private keys, much more secure and robust.

In fact, this infrastructure is a very sophisticated form of asymmetric cryptography, and it is known as the public key infrastructure (PKI). The basic premise of PKI is to help create, organize, store, distribute, and maintain the public keys. But in this infrastructure, both of the private and public keys are referred to as digital signatures, and they are not created by the sending and receiving parties; rather, they created by a separate entity known as the certificate authority.

This entity is usually an outside third party that hosts the technological infrastructure needed to initiate, create, and distribute the digital certificates. In a very macro view, the PKI consists of the following components:

1. The certificate authority (CA): This is the outside third party who issues the digital certificates.
2. The digital certificate: As mentioned, this consists of both the private key and the public key, which are issued by the CA. This is also the entity that the end user would go to in case he or she needed to have a digital certificate verified. These digital certificates are typically kept in the local computer of the employee, or even the central server at the organization.
3. The LDAP or X.500 directories: These are the databases that collect and distribute the digital certificates from the CA.
4. The registration authority (RA): If the organization is very large (such as a multinational corporation), this entity usually handles the requests for the required digital certificates and then transmits those requests to the CA to process and create the required digital certificates.

In terms of the CA, in extremely simple terms, it can be viewed as the main governing body, or even the "king" of the PKI. In order to start using the PKI to communicate with others, it is the CA that issues the digital certificates, which consist of both the public and private keys.

The Digital Certificates

Each digital certificate which is generated by the Certificate Authority consists of the following technical specifications:

1. The Digital Certificate Version Number: Typically, it is either version number 1, 2, or 3.
2. The Serial Number: This is the unique ID number that separates and distinguishes a particular digital certificate from all of the others (this can be likened to each digital certificate having its own Social Security number).
3. The Signature Algorithm Identifier: This contains the information and data about the mathematical algorithm used by the CA to issue the particular digital certificate.
4. The Issuer Name: This is the actual name of the CA that is issuing the digital certificate to the organization.
5. The Validity Period: This contains both the activation and deactivation dates of the digital certificates; in other words, this is the lifetime of the digital certificate as determined by the CA.
6. The Public Key: This is created by the CA.

7. The Subject Distinguished Name: This is the name that specifies the digital certificate owner.
8. The Subject Alternate Name Email: This specifies the digital certificate's owner email address (this is where the actual digital certificates go to).
9. The Subject Name URL: This is the web address of the organization to whom the digital certificates are issued.

How the Public Key Infrastructure Works

This is how the first part of the PKI works:

1. The request for the digital certificate is sent to the appropriate CA.
2. After this request has been processed, the digital certificate is issued to the person who is requesting it.
3. The digital certificate then gets signed by confirming the actual identity of the person who is requesting it.
4. The digital certificate can now be used to encrypt the plaintext into the ciphertext, which is sent from the sending party to the receiving party.

The RA is merely a subset of the CA; it is not intended to replace or take over the role of the CA, but instead, it is designed to help if it becomes overwhelmed with digital certificate request traffic. The RA by itself does not grant any type of digital certificate, nor does it confirm the identity of the person who is requesting the digital certificate. Rather, its role is to help process the requests until the processing queue at the CA becomes much more manageable.

The RA sends all of the digital certificate requests in one big batch, rather than one at a time. This process is known as "chaining certificates." The RA is typically found in very large, multinational corporations, where each office location would have its own RA and the CA would reside at the main corporate headquarters.

Finally, all digital certificate requests processed by the RA are also associated with a chain of custody trail for security auditing purposes. The RA can be viewed as a support vehicle for the CA in which a mathematical, hierarchal relationship exists.

Public Key Infrastructure Policies and Rules

It should be noted at this point that in order for either the CA or the RA to function properly, it is important to have a distinct set of rules and policies in place. These surround the use of the issuance, storage, and revocation of the expired digital certificate. While it is beyond the scope of this book to get into the exact details of all these rules and policies, the following is just a sampling of some of the topics that need to be addressed:

1. Where and how the records and the audit logs of the CA are to be kept, stored, and archived
2. The administrative roles for the CA
3. Where and how the public keys and the private keys are to be kept, stored, and backed up
4. The length of time for which the public keys and the private keys will be stored
5. If public or private key recovery will be allowed by the CA
6. The length of the validity period for both the public keys and private keys
7. The technique whereby the CA can delegate the responsibilities to the RA
8. If the digital certificates issued by the CA will be used for applications and resources
9. If the digital certificates issued by the CA will be used for the sole purpose of encrypting the ciphertext
10. If there are any types of applications that should be refused digital certificates
11. When a digital certificate is initially authorized by the CA, if there will be a finite period when the digital certificate will be subject to revocation

As one can see, based upon the establishment of the many rules and policies that need to be set in place, the actual deployment and establishment of a PKI can become quite complex, depending upon the size and the need of the particular business or organization.

The LDAP Protocol

In terms of the database structure for the digital certificates, this is most useful and effective when LDAP servers are utilized. LDAP is simply a database protocol that is used for the updating and searching of the directories which run over the Transmission Control Protocol/Internet Protocol (TCP/IP) network protocol (this is the network protocol that is primarily used by the PKI).

It is the job of the LDAP server of the PKI to contain the information and data that relate to the digital certificates, the public and the private key storage locations, and the matching public and private key labels.

The CA uses a combination of the end-user name and the matching tags to specifically locate the digital certificates on the LDAP server. From that point, the LDAP server checks to see if the requested digital certificate is valid or not, and it if it is valid, it retrieves from its database a digital certificate which can then be sent to the end user. Although all digital certificates that are issued have a finite lifespan when they are first issued, they can also be revoked for any reason at any time by the PKI administrator.

In order to accomplish this specific task, a certificate revocation list (CRL) is used. This list is composed of the digital certificate serial numbers that have been assigned by the CA. But looking this type of information and data can be very taxing on system resources and processes. Therefore, it is obviously much easier to reissue the digital certificates as they expire, rather than revoke them and having to reissue them again, and of course, this would mean that the PKI system administrator would then have to update the CRL.

The Public Cryptography Standards

The PKI is governed by a body known as the Public Key Cryptography Standards (PKCS). The first of these standards were previously described, and they are the RSA encryption standard, the Diffie-Hellman key agreement standard, and the elliptical wave theory. The other sets of standards that define a PKI are as follows:

1. The Password-Based Cryptography Standard: This describes how to encrypt a private key with a secret key that is derived from a password.
2. The Extended Certificate Syntax Standard: This is merely a set of attributes attached to a digital certificate that has been assigned by the CA.
3. The Cryptographic Message Syntax Standard: This standard specifically outlines how to put the digital signatures into digital certificate envelopes, and from there, put that into another digital envelope.
4. The Private Key Information Syntax Standard: This standard directly specifies what kind of information and data should be included into a private key and how that specific key should be formatted.
5. The Selected Attribute Type: This is a detailed list that describes the certain encryption attribute types for the last three standards.
6. The Certification Request Syntax Standard: This provides the details for the syntax for the digital certificates. Essentially, this standard simply sets forth the parameters that are needed for the CA to understand the digital certificate request.
7. The Cryptographic Token Interface Standard: This is an application programming interface (API) for specifying and handling the cryptographic functions as it relates to smartcards.
8. The Personal Information Exchange Standard: This standard specifies exactly how an end user's private keys should be transported across the network medium.
9. The Cryptographic Token Information Format Standard: This standard specifies how the applications at an organization should interface with smartcards.

In the world of the PKI, it should be remembered that the public keys and the private keys (also known as the digital certificates) are created instantaneously and all of the time. In fact, public keys and private keys are everywhere in a PKI, even when one establishes a Secure Shell (SSH) connection over the Internet with their particular brand of web browser (this typically uses 128-bit encryption).

In fact, there are even public keys and private keys in the PKI that are only used once, terminated, and discarded. These types of public keys and private keys are known more commonly as session keys. Public keys and private keys are nothing more than computer files.

Parameters of Public Keys and Private Keys

Before the actual public key or the private key can go out, it needs to have certain parameters, and these are as follows:

1. The type of mathematical algorithm which should be used (as described previously)
2. How many bits of data the public keys and the private keys should be composed of
3. The expiration date of both the public keys and the private keys

Also, in order to keep hackers at bay, it is equally important that not all of the public keys and the private keys be used all the time in the communication process between the sending and the receiving parties. It is also important to keep the public keys and the private keys fresh, or in other words, it is important to introduce randomness into the PKI.

Such randomness is known as entropy, and this entropy is created by what are known as random number generators and pseudo-random number generators. Also, in a PKI, there are different classes of public keys and private keys. Here is a listing of just some of these classes:

1. Signing Keys: These are the keys to create the digital signatures.
2. Authentication Keys: These are the keys that are created to authenticate computers, servers, and the receiving parties and the sending parties with one another.
3. Data Encryption Keys: These are the keys that are used to encrypt the files.
4. Session Keys: These are the keys that are used to help secure a channel across an entire network for only a very short period.
5. Key Encryption Keys: These types of keys literally wrap the ciphertext to provide further protection between the sending and the receiving parties.
6. Reof Key: This is the master that is used for signing all of the other public keys and private keys which originate specifically from the CA.

How Many Servers?

In the PKI, especially in small to medium sized businesses, very often only one server is utilized in order to distribute both the public keys and the private keys to the employees within the organization. But the primary disadvantage with this is these types of key servers can literally become a single point of failure if the server breaks down, or worse yet, it is hacked into.

In order to help alleviate this problem, these types of business can have multiple, redundant servers, but this, too, can become a huge expense, especially for the small to medium sized business. Thus, as a result, the best option for the small to medium sized businesses, as well as even the large multinational corporations, is to outsource to a third party the entire PKI, such as with such organizations as Verisign.

This approach can be considered a hosted one and can greatly save on IT-related expenses, and security is at the forefront of these hosting parties. Another important issue that is related to that of public key and private key distribution in a PKI is the setting of security policies for both the public keys and the private keys and which mechanisms are used for their storage, as well as furthering the securing of the public keys and the private keys themselves (this is a topic for what is known as virtual private networks [VPNs], and this will be discussed in the next major section of this chapter).

Security Policies

The exact mechanism as to how to exactly establish a specific security policy is beyond the scope of this book, but the security policy should cover, at a minimum, the following key issues as it relates to public key and private key generation and distribution:

1. The individuals who are authorized to access the key server (assuming that the place of business or organization has one)
2. Who within the organization is even allowed to use the public keys and the private keys at all
3. What types of ciphertexts and content messages and even corporate data can use the encryption methods provided by the public and the private keys
4. If the public key and private key generation and distribution processes are outsourced to a third party, who at the organization has the authority to issue public keys and private keys after they have been generated
5. The specific requirements for the employees within the organization to obtain both public keys and private keys

Securing the Public Keys and the Private Keys

Related to the issue of public key and private key security is how to secure the keys themselves. Broadly speaking, there are two ways in which this can be handled:

1. Key escrow
2. Key recovery

Key escrow refers to the storage of the public keys and the private keys at a safe location, and key recovery refers to breaking up the public keys and the private keys at the point of origin (which would be when the ciphertext is sent from the sending party) and putting them back together once again at the point of destination (which would be when the receiving party receives the ciphertext).

Message Digests and Hashes

However, in today's business world, both of these methods are totally infeasible due to security concerns. Today, the method preferred by most chief information officers (CIOs) is using message digests and hashes. Both of these refer to the same concept and are often used synonymously with each other. Essentially, it is a fixed length of literally data nonsense, such as:

```
RTYHDHDHjjjdd8585858hd0909344jdjdjdjMNGDfsweqwecbthrdn*&^%gh$
```

This helps ensure the integrity of the ciphertext while it is in transit across the network medium. In other words, this is proof positive for the receiving party who receives the ciphertext from the sending party that the ciphertext has remained intact while it has been in transit and it has not been altered in any way, shape, or form.

The hash or the message digest can be viewed as a fingerprint of the ciphertext. The hash is actually created at the point of receiving party, and it is then calculated again via a mathematical algorithm utilized by the receiving party. If the mathematical algorithm used by the receiving party generates the same type of garbled data message such as the one shown in the example, the receiving party can be 100% sure that the ciphertext they have received from the sending party is the original ciphertext at the point of origination and has remained intact.

Security Vulnerabilities of Hashes

However, a major security vulnerability of using hashes is that they can be altered while en route. In other words, a hacker can intercept the ciphertext and its associated hash, alter both, and create a brand-new ciphertext and a brand-new hash. As a result, the receiving party is fooled into believing that this new, altered cipher-text and the new altered hash are the originals sent by the sending party, while the hacker keeps the actual ciphertext and hash that was generated the first time around.

To fix this major security vulnerability, the ciphertext is combined with a "secret key" at the point of origination first, and then the hash is created. As a result, this hash will contain specific information and data about the secret key itself. In turn, the receiving party can be further ensured that the ciphertext they have received is the original sent by the sending party. This is so because even if the ciphertext, the hash, and the associated secret key were to be intercepted, there is very little that a hacker can do to alter the ciphertext and its associated hash, because they need the information and data about the secret key, which is, of course, something they will never gain access to.

A Technical Review of Cryptography

The last subsections of this chapter provided an in-depth introduction to cryptography, albeit at a higher level. Of course, it gets much more complicated than that, and getting into every detail is beyond the scope of this chapter. But in this part, we will provide a "deeper dive" into the various elements of cryptography, especially in those areas that relate to securing the web application and the server that it resides upon.

We first start by exploring more into the technical aspects of the DES.

The Digital Encryption Standard

The DES consists primarily of two separate components:

1. Confusion:
   This the part of the DES in which the relationship between the key that is being used (either public or private) and the ciphertext that it is protecting becomes invisible to the outside world. This type of association can be typically found wherever the substitution principle is needed in securing the confidential information and data that resides upon the web application server.
2. Diffusion:
   This is an encryption process where the characters used in the plaintext message are actually distributed over many other ciphertext-based symbols that are used to mask it from the outside world. A common element that is used here is known as bit permutation.

It is important to note that simply using confusion and diffusion separately will not provide ample enough security for the web application or the server that it resides upon. Rather, the two need to be used in conjunction with one another in order to build a strong cipher that cannot be easily broken into by the cyberattacker. Combining both confusion and diffusion is known as the product cipher.

In fact, any modern block cipher, but especially DES, possesses high-level properties that are based upon diffusion. For example, moving around a bit of a plaintext message will result in the change of at least half of the output bits that have been formulated. In other words, the second half of the ciphertext that has been create from the plaintext message is statistically independent of the first half of the output bits that have been created. This is a crucial aspect of the DES.

The DES is a cipher that has the capability to encrypt blocks of plaintext messages that are at least 64 bits in length and possesses a key size of 56 bits. It is also what is known as a symmetric cipher, which means that the same key is very often used for both encrypting and decrypting the plaintext message. It is essentially an iterative-based mathematical algorithm, which simply means that for each block of a plaintext message that needs to be protected, the level of encryption that is provided is accomplished in 16 distinctive rounds.

In each of these 16 separate rounds, a unique subkey is created and utilized (which can be denoted as "Ki") from the main key (which can be denoted as "K"). Most of the time, the DES makes use of what is known technically as the Feistel network. One of the key advantages of utilizing this is that both the encryption and the decryption processes can be conducted by using the same operation.

For example, the decryption of the Feistel network only needs what is known as a reversed key schedule. This can provide strong advantages in terms of protecting both the web application and its server. Here is how the Feistel network carries out its operations:

1. An internal bitwise permutation (known as "IP") is used to encrypt a plaintext message that is at least 64 bits in length.
2. Then, the plaintext message is split into two separate halves, which are referred to as "Lo" and "Ro," respectively.
3. These are then fed into the Feistel network, which will provide for 16 rounds (or layers) of encryption.
4. The right half (referred to as "Ri") is fed into a function known simply as "f."
5. The output of this computed function is then statistically XOR'ed with the left half of the Feistel network, which is 32 bits length, and is represented as "Li."
6. Once these two steps have been accomplished, the process just outlined is transposed, and this keeps continuing until full encryption can be completely realized.

Mathematically, this entire process can be represented as follows:

$$Li = Ri - 1;$$
$$Ri = Li \text{ XOR } f(Ri - 1, ki)$$

where i = all of the rounds from the starting point of 1 to the ending point of 16.

It is important to note that the final permutation, which is round 16, can be represented as IP ^ –1. This is actually the last round of processing from within the DES. The key schedule also manages and maintains each of the 16 rounds.

Also, the Feistel network provides encryption initially in the first half of the input bits in each of the successive 16 rounds, which is at the left side of the particular input. In order to start the encryption process for the right side of the Feistel network, it is literally copied to the next round (which at first would be round 2).

Finally, the confusion and diffusion properties, as described before, can only be achieved from within the f-based function. The Feistel network actually becomes more secure as the processing of each of the 16 rounds is completed.

The Internal Structure of the DES

The actual internal structure of the DES is further examined in this subsection, and contains the following components:

- The initial and final permutations
- The f-function
- The key schedule

The Initial and Final Permutations

The initial permutation is represented as IP and the final permutation is represented as IP ^ –1. These are both considered bitwise mathematical permutations and have been created and deployed in order to categorize the plaintext, ciphertext, and its related bits into a byte-wise scheme. The premise of this is to make the encryption and the decryption processes as seamless as possible.

The f-Function

This functionality plays a very critical role in securing the DES. For instance, in round "i" (of the 16 total rounds that are available, as previously described), it usually takes the right half of $R_i – 1$ from the output of the previous round, as well as the current round key that is being used, "k_i," as the input. As a result, the output of the f-function is then statistically XOR'ed in order to encrypt the left half of the round, which is denoted as "$l_i – 1$."

The mathematical structure of the f-function is represented as a 32-bit input, which can be expanded out to 48 bits. This is done by partitioning the input into eight different 4-bit blocks, and from there, expanding each of the blocks into 6 bits. This type of permutation consists of 4 bits (which are 1, 2, 3, and 4, respectively) in the first block. In succession, the second block consists of 4 bits (which are 5, 6, 7, and 8, respectively).

Once the result of 48 bits has been achieved, the expansion is then statistically XOR'ed with any round key that is available, which is represented as "ki." From here, the eight 6-bit blocks are then are divided up into what are known as substitution boxes (S-boxes), in which there are eight of them in total. This is what actually defines the overall cryptographic strength of the DES. In fact, the S-box is the only nonlinear component that exists in the DES algorithm.

This nonlinearity can be expressed mathematically as follows:

$$S(a)\, XOR\ S(b) = /\ S(a\ XOR\ b)$$

Interestingly, if this nonlinearity did not exist in the DES, it is quite possible that it could be hacked into by a cyberattacker. In the end, the 32-bit output that has been created is permuted in a bit-wise fashion. The mathematical diffusion that is introduced by the S-box is known technically as the avalanche effect.

The Key Schedule

This component of the DES makes use of 16 round keys, which can be represented once again as "ki." Each of them consists of 48 bits, based upon the original 56-bit key. It should be noted at this point that these distinct round keys can also be referred to as subkeys. They are usually expressed as 64 bits in length, in which every eighth bit can be utilized as "odd parity" against the preceding seven bits. Keep in mind that the eighth bit does not possess a separate key value and does not add any value in terms of security enhancement to the DES algorithm.

Because of this, the overall 64-bit key is then reduced to 56 bits by discarding every eighth bit. From this point, the 56-bit key is mathematically split into two halves, which are represented as "Co" and "Do," respectively. The 56-bit key then becomes two 28 bits (Co and Do), which are rotated out to the left by one or two positions, which is dependent solely upon the round "I."

This positioning is dictated by the following parameters:

■ In the rounds of where i = 1, 2, 9, and 16, the two halves are shifted to the left by one bit.
■ In the other successive rounds in which i =/1, 2, 9, and 16, respectively, the two halves are shifted by two bits.

These parameters only apply to either of the two 28-bit halves. Thus, the total number of the rotation positions can be mathematically represented as follows:

$$4*1+12*2 = 28$$

OR

$$where\ Co = C16\ and\ where\ Do = D16$$

This mathematical property is actually needed for the decryption process of the DES algorithm to occur.

The Decryption Process of the DES Algorithm

As mentioned earlier in this section, one of the primary advantages of the DES algorithm is that the decryption process is virtually the same as the encryption process, because the primary framework of the DES is the Feistel network. In this subsection, we look at two types of decryption components that are associated with the DES algorithm:

- The reversed key schedule
- The decryption in the Feistel network

The Reversed Key Schedule

In this particular process, the key question that needs to be asked is if you have an initial key of "k," how possible is it to generate a key of "k16"? It was examined earlier that $Co = C16$ and $Do = D16$. Thus, the key of "k16" can be mathematically derived after $PC - 1$, which is demonstrated as follows:

$$K16 = PC - 2(C16, D16)$$
$$= PC - 2 \ (Co, Do)$$
$$= PC - [2(PC - 1(k)]$$

In order to compute the key of "k15," the intermediate variables of C15 and D15 are needed. These can be also mathematically derived from (C16,D16). But it should be noted that this can only be done via a right shift, and this is mathematically represented as:

$$K15 = PC - 2(C15,D15)$$
$$= PC - 2[RS2(C16), RS2(D16)]$$
$$= PC - 2[RS2(Co), RS2(Do0)]$$

These rounds keep continuing, via the right-shift approach, until the key of "k1" is reached.

The Decryption in the Feistel Network

With this process, the decryption in round 1 actually reverses the encryption in round 16, the decryption in round 2 reverses the encryption that has occurred in round 15, etc. This cycle keeps continuing until the reversal of the encryption in round 1 has been reached. This is mathematically represented as:

$$(Lo^\wedge d,\ Ro^\wedge d) = IP(Y) = IP[IP^\wedge\text{-}1(R16, L160)] = (R16,\ L16)$$

where:

$Lo^\wedge d = R16$

$Ro^\wedge d = R15$

It is important to note at this point that the decryption subprocess is notated by the superscript of "d" and that the encryption subprocess does not possess any type of superscript. The previous equation shows that the input from the first round of the decryption subprocess is equal to the last round of the encryption subprocess. In other words, the first round of the decryption subprocess merely cancels out the last round of the encryption subprocess.

To accomplish this particular task, the output values of $(L1^\wedge d, R1^\wedge d)$ have to be mathematically associated with the decryption subprocess in terms of the last encryption round (L15, R15). This association can be mathematically represented as follows:

$$L1^\wedge d = Ro^\wedge d = L16 = R15$$

Further, this is how $R1^\wedge d$ is mathematically computed:

$$R1^\wedge d = Lo^\wedge d\ XOR\ f\ (Ro^\wedge d, k16) = R16\ XOR\ f(L16, k16)$$

$$R1^\wedge d = L15\ XOR\ f\ (R15, k16) = R16\ XOR\ f(R15, k16)$$

$$R1^\wedge d = L15\ XOR\ f\ (R15, k16) = R16\ XOR\ f(R15, k16) = L15$$

It is the last mathematical equation that is the most crucial. For example, a duplicate f-function is XOR'ed in two distinct patterns to L15. As a result, both of these subprocesses cancel each other out, so that $R1^\wedge d = L15$ in the end. Because of this, we now have proven that the first decryption round reverses or cancels out the last encryption round. As mentioned previously, this subprocess will keep going on until all of the 15 decryption rounds have been examined. Mathematically, this can be represented as follows:

$$L1^\wedge d = R16 - i;$$

$$R1^\wedge d = L16 - i$$

where i = the total number of iterations.

Finally, once all 16 decryption subprocesses have been analyzed, the entire process as just detailed is completely reversed. The mathematical equation for this is as follows:

$$IP^\wedge\text{-}1(R^\wedge 16,\ L16^\wedge d) = Ip^\wedge\text{-}1(Lo,\ Ro) = IP^\wedge\text{-}1\ [IP(x)] = x$$

where x = the plaintext that was used as the input initially in the DES algorithm.

The Security of the DES

So far, the DES algorithm has proven to be more or less resistant to cyberattacks. But on a theoretical level, two types of cyberattacks could pose a major threat to it, which are:

- The differential cryptanalysis
- The linear cryptanalysis

Research has shown that a cyberattacker needs at least 2^{47} plaintext–cipher pairs in order to launch a successful differential cryptanalysis attack. Likewise, in order to launch a linear cryptanalysis attack, he or she would need at least 2^{43} plaintext–cipher pairs. But it is quite unlikely in reality that a cyberattacker would actually launch these kinds of attacks against the DES algorithm for the following reasons:

- The cyberattacker needs to possess a lot of knowledge about the number of plaintext messages.
- Collecting all of this information and data will take a very long time, and thus requires a large amount of both memory and processing resources.
- In these instances, the cyberattacker can only recover one plaintext-cipher key.

The Advanced Encryption Standard

The next important cryptographic algorithm used to secure the web application and the server that it resides on is AES. A key component of this algorithm is the block cipher known as the Rindjael. The respective block and key size can vary anywhere from 128 to 256 bits, depending upon the type of application that it is being used for. This is a significant improvement over the DES algorithm (as reviewed extensively in the last section), which allowed for only 128 bits.

It is important to note that the AES algorithm, the separate keys must be used (whether it is exclusively public or private, or even a combination of both) and the number of internal rounds that take are is purely a mathematical function of the key length, as just reviewed. Also, the DES algorithm does not possess a Feisal structure, as opposed to the DES algorithm, which does. Also in comparison to the DES algorithm, the AES algorithm can encrypt the plaintext up to 128 bits in one single round; the DES can only encrypt 32 bits in each round.

The AES algorithm is composed of three separate and distinct layers, which are also often referred to as the data paths. They are as follows:

1. The Key Addition Layer:
   This can be the 128- to 256-bit keys, and they all have been derived from the primary key, which is located in the master key schedule. These keys, as described, are then XOR'ed to a primary state of function.

2. The Byte Submission Layer:

This is also known as the S-box, which was reviewed in detail in the last subsection. At this particular level, each of the 128- to 256-bit keys are nonlinearly transformed by using various mathematical "look-up" algorithms. This procedure adds what is known as mathematical confusion to the plaintext that is being encrypted, which ensures that any changes made to it remain intact by using various hashing-based formulas.

3. The Diffusion Layer:

This specialized procedure allows for diffusion to transpire over the 128- to 256-bit keys. This layer also consists of two sublayers, which are as follows:

- The ShiftRows: This allows for various types of permutations to take place on the plaintext on the 128- to 256-bit keys.
- The MixColumn layer: This is a linear algebra-based matrix procedure that can combine blocks of plaintext 4 bytes at a time.

Also, the DES algorithm, in a manner similar to that of the AES algorithm, can compute any round key or subkey as (Ko, K1, K2, etc.).

The Mathematics behind the DES Algorithm

The main mathematical foundation for the DES algorithm is known as Galois fields, and it consists of the following:

- Finite fields
- Prime fields
- Extension fields
- Sophisticated addition and subtraction
- Sophisticated multiplication
- Inversions in GF (2^m)

These are now examined in greater detail:

1. The Existence of Finite Fields:

It should be noted that finite fields can also be referred to as a Galois field. This is a numerical set of information and data with a finite grouping of particular elements. From within this, complex addition, subtraction, multiplication, and geometric inversions can take place. More specifically, a group can be defined as one set of operations along with its corresponding, inverse operation. For example, if the procedure to be carried is addition, then the inverse operation would be, of course, subtraction. Likewise, if the procedure to be carried out is multiplication, then the inverse operation would be division. In order to have all four of these mathematical operations in one structure, a specific set is then needed, which is called a field. The number of elements in the Galois field is also called the cardinality. The mathematical theorem that establishes the foundation for the Galois field is as follows:

> A field with order 'm' only exists if 'm' is a prime power, where m = p^n. In this case, 'n' is a positive integer, and 'p' is a prime integer. 'p' is also referred as the characteristic of the finite field.[3]

In other words, when there is a finite field that consists of 11, 81 (where 81 = 3^4), or 256 elements (where 256 = 2^8), there is no finite field with just 12 elements, because 12 = 2^2 * 3, and 12 is not a prime number.

2. The Prime Fields:

   Probably the best examples of the finite field are those where the fields consist of a distinct prime order, where n = 1. The elements in this kind of field can be denoted as integers of 0, 1, and p − 1. The two types that can be conducted in this field are known as modular integer addition and integer multiplication with the modulo P. This is based upon the following mathematical theorem:

   > P is a prime number. There exists an Integer Ring known as 'Zp', and this is represented as GF(p), and is also known as a prime field, or a Galois Field, which consists of a prime number of elements. Any elements that are non-zero in nature in the GF(p) will automatically have an inverse operation that is associated with it. Any mathematical calculations are done via the Modulo P.[3]

   In other words, if the integer ring of Z^m consists of any integers with a modular-based addition and multiplication property, and if 'm' is a prime number, then Z^m can also be considered as a finite field. In order to do any sort of mathematical calculations in the prime field, the following integer ring rules must be followed:

   – Any addition or multiplication operations are carried out with the modulo P, where the additive inverse can be referred to as:

   $$a + (-a) = \text{mod 'p'}$$

   – The multiplicative inverse can be represented as follows:

   $$a * a^{-1} = 1$$

   It should be noted that another crucial prime field in this instance is that of GF(2) = (0,1), where any mathematical calculations are done with the modulo 2.

3. The Extension Fields:

   In the AES algorithm, any finite field consists of at least 256 elements, and this can be represented as "GF (2^28)." In this, each of the elements are represented by just 1 byte of information or data. In other words, the AES algorithm considers each and every byte as an element of the field GF (2^28), and any sort of mathematical manipulations are done from within this finite field. But if the order of the finite field is not prime, then these are referred to as extension fields, where m > 1. The elements here can be represented by the use of polynomials and can be mathematically represented as follows:

$$A(x) = a7x^7 + \ldots a1x + a0, \text{ where } Ai = GF(2) = \{0,1\}$$

In this instance, 256 distinct polynomial groupings are possible, and can be stored as an 8-bit vector as follows:

$$A = (a7, a6, a5, a4, a3, a2, a1, a0)$$

4. Sophisticated Addition and Subtraction:
   It should be noted that the key addition layer in the AES algorithm makes use of additive properties. Addition is achieved by the following:

$$C(x) = A(x) + B(x) = \Sigma(m-1)(i = 0)CiX^1, Ci = Ai + Bi \text{ Mod } 2$$

Subtraction is achieved by the following:

$$C(x) = A(x) - B(x) = \Sigma(m-1)(i = 0)CiX^1, Ci = Ai - Bi = Ai + Bi \text{ Mod } 2$$

5. Sophisticated Multiplication:
   Any sort of multiplicative operations carried out in the AES algorithm makes use of the MixColumn transformation procedures and polynomials in a finite field. This is mathematically represented as:

$$A(x) * B(x) = (Am-1x^{m-1} + \ldots + Ao) * (Bm-1x^{m-1} + \ldots + Bo)$$
$$C'(x) = c'2m-2^x^2m-2 + \ldots C'o$$

where:

$$C'o = AoBo \text{ Mod2}$$
$$C'1 = AoB1 + A1Bo \text{ Mod2}$$
$$C'2m-2 = Am-1^Bm-1 \text{Mod2}$$

It is also important to note that the AES algorithm makes use of what are known as irreducible polynomials, and are mathematically represented as follows:

$$P(x) = x^8 + x^4 + x^3 + x + 1$$

6. Inversions in GF (2^m):

This is considered a crucial property in the AES algorithm. This can also be mathematically represented as follows:

$$A^{-1}(x) * A(x) = 1 \, Mod \, P(x)$$

The Internal Structure of the AES Algorithm

The AES algorithm consists of the following layers:

- The byte substitution layer
- The diffusion layer
- The key addition layer

It should be noted at this point that the AES algorithm is actually a byte-oriented cipher, unlike the DES algorithm, which makes extensive usage of bit permutations, thus giving it the bit-oriented infrastructure.

These will now be reviewed in further detail.

1. The Byte Substitution Layer:

This is considered the first layer of the internal structure of the AES algorithm. This is mathematically represented as a row of 16 parallel S-boxes, with each box containing 8 input and 8 output bits. Unlike the DES algorithm, where only eight different S-boxes are used, the AES algorithm S-boxes are all identical. This can be represented by the following formula:

$$S(Ai) = Bi$$

where state byte Ai is replaced by another state byte, Bi. It should be noted that the S-box is the only component in the AES algorithm that is not linear in nature. For example:

$$ByteSub(A) + ByteSub(B) = /ByteSub(A + B)$$

The technical mapping of the S-box substitution (as just described) is done via bijective mapping. In other words, each of the $2^8 = 256$ inputs is matched up on a one-to-one basis to each output element. This unique feature allows the S-box to be reversed, which is a crucial component that is needed in order to decrypt the AES algorithm. Another key component of the AES algorithm is the GF (2^28) functionality. Because of its nonlinearity properties, it affords a strong level of protection against cyberthreats that are posed to the AES algorithm.

2. The Diffusion Layer:
This layer of the AES algorithm consists of two different sublayers, which are described as follows:
  - The ShiftRows Sublayer: Using a cyclical approach, this mechanism shifts the second row of the state matrix by 3 bytes to the right, the third row by 2 bytes at a time to the right, and finally, the fourth row by 1 byte to the right. The ultimate goal of these shifting processes is to further enhance the diffusion properties of the AES algorithm.
  - The MixColumn Sublayer: This is actually a linear-based transformation which integrates, or mixes, each column of the state matrix. In this particular instance, each and every input byte has a direct influence over the four corresponding out bytes. This sublayer is deemed to be the major diffusion component of the AES algorithm. In fact, it is the combination of these two sublayers that it makes it possible to have just three rounds where each and every byte of the state matrix can produce 16 plaintext bytes. This can be represented as follows:

$$\text{MixColumn } (B) = C$$

where:

$B = $ Input State

$C = $ Output State

Keep in mind that, as discussed in the last subsection, the concept of diffusion is literally spreading the influence as to how individual bits are calculated over an entire state. This sublayer does not consist of an S-box that is nonlinear in nature; rather, it makes use of state matrices.

3. The Key Addition Layer:
This internal part of the AES algorithm takes the input key that was first derived (these are the 128, 192, and 256 bits as discussed earlier), and from there, derives the subkeys that are used in the AES algorithm. The XOR process is utilized here, and it can also be referred to as "key whitening." In this situation, the total number of subkeys is equal to the total number of rounds that were needed to process them, plus one extra round.
    The total number of rounds for each bit size is as follows:
  - 128 Bits: 10 rounds are needed ($Nr = 10$) and 11 subkeys are generated, which has a key length of 128 bits.
  - 192 Bits: 10 rounds are needed ($Nr = 10$) and 13 subkeys are generated, which has a key length of 128 bits.
  - 256 Bits: 10 rounds are needed ($Nr = 10$) and 15 subkeys are generated, which has a key length of 128 bits.

These subkeys are produced recursively, and it is important to note that the AES key schedule is what is known as "word-oriented." In this case, one word is equal to 32 bits. There are different schedules for the 128 bits, 192 bits, and 256 bits, which are as follows:

- The Key Schedule for the 128-Bit Key:
  The 11 subkeys are stored in a key expansion array, with the individual elements represented as follows:

$$W[0\}, \ldots W[43]$$

The first subkey (k0) is actually the original AES algorithm key, and this is then transferred to the first four elements of the key array (W). The other elements are calculated as follows, based upon this mathematical formula:

$$W[4i] = W[4(i\text{-}1)] + g(W[4i\text{-}1])$$

'g' is a nonlinear functionality, which consists of a 4-byte input and output. It is computed recursively as follows:

$$W[4i+j] = W[4i+j-1] + W[4(i\text{-}1)+j]$$

where $i = 1$ through 10 and $j = 1, 2,$ and 3.

- The Key Schedule for the 192-Bit Key:
  This particular schedule has 12 distinct rounds, with 11 subkeys of 128 bits each. These subkeys require at a minimum 52 "words," and are thus stored in the array element represented as $W[0] \ldots W[51]$. The formulation of this array element is virtually the same as the process just described for the 128-bit keys. In this schedule, eight iterations are used, and are represented as follows:

    (W[0], W[1], W[2], W[3]) for the first round;

    (W[4], W[5], W[6], W[7]) for the second round.

These representations keep going until all eight iterations are completed.

- The Key Schedule for the 256-Bit Key:
  This particular schedule has 15 subkeys, each with 256-bit keys. It consists of seven distinct iterations, which are calculated in the same fashion as just described. There are also seven round coefficients, which are represented as follows:

$$RC[1] \ldots RC[7]$$

This schedule also has a distinct functionality represented as "h()." It consists of a 4-byte input and output, and even applies to the S-box, as previously described.

It is important to note that two different techniques can be used when implementing the 128-bit key, 192-bit key, and 256-bit key schedules, as follows:

– Precomputation:

With this technique, all of the subkeys are expanded into the array denoted as "W." The encryption and decryption process making use of the AES algorithm takes place after this expansion fully occurs.

– On the Fly:

With this procedure, a new subkey is created for each and every new round during the encryption and decryption processes. In the decryption phase, the last subkey is XOR'ed with the ciphertext that has been created. Thus, all of the subkeys are first derived in a recursive fashion, and then the decryption process starts off the ciphertext with subsequent "on the fly" generation of the various subkeys.

Decryption of the AES Algorithm

It is important to note at this point that the AES algorithm does not make use of the Feistel network, as does the DES algorithm. A unique property about the former is that it must be inverted; for example:

■ The Byte Substitution layer becomes the Inv Byte Substitution layer.
■ The ShiftRows layer becomes the Inv Shift layer.
■ The MixColumn layer becomes the Inv MixColumn layer.

Also, the order of the subkeys is reversed, because the last round of encryption in the AES algorithm does not calculate the MixColumn layer and the first decryption round will not contain an inverse layer. But all of the other rounds will contain some sort of AES layer.

1. The Inverse MixColumn Substitution Layer:

In this particular process, the addition of the subkey is applied to the state matrix. In order to get the reverse of the MixColumn, an inverse matrix must be applied. This is a 4-bit matrix, which is then mathematically multiplied by the inverse of the 4×4 matrix. This matrix also consists of constant values, which do not change over time. Any further multiplication and addition that are needed of these values (also referred to as "coefficients") are carried out in the $GF(2^8)$ functionality. The second column of the state matrix contains the output bytes (B4, B5, B6, B7), which are then computed by multiplying the four input bytes (C4, C5, C6, C7) in a repetitive fashion. The constant values in the state matrix are in a hexadecimal format, which is mathematically represented as follows:

$$0B = (0B)hex = (00001011)^2 = x^3 + x + 1$$

The addition computations are done by using bitwise XOR operations.

2. The Inverse ShiftRows Substitution Layer:

In order to get the reverse of this, the rows are shifted in the state matrix in an opposite format. The first row in this matrix does not change, but the others do, which is represented as follows:

$$B = (B0, B1, \ldots. B15)$$

3. The Inverse Byte Substitution Layer:

In order to get the inverse of this layer, the S-box is used when the ciphertext is in the decryption process. The S-box in the AES algorithm is bijective in nature, and is the inverse of the S-box, which is computed as follows:

$$Ai = S^{-1}(Bi) = S^{-1}[S(Ai)]$$

The second step of the inverse of the Galois field is also calculated, with following formula:

$$Ai = (B'i)^{-1} = GF(2^8)$$

And the following "fixed reduction" polynomial is used as well:

$$P(x) = X^8, + X^4 + X^3 + X + 1$$

Asymmetric and Public Key Cryptography

In the world of cryptography, there are two types of systems: symmetric cryptography and asymmetric cryptography. With the former, only one key is used, which is the private key, for both encryption and decryption purposes. While this has certain advantages to it (such as minimal computational and processing power is needed), there is a huge disadvantage to it. If the private key were to be compromised, a third party would have easy access to the ciphertext.

But with asymmetric cryptography, two keys are used, which is the public key and the private key. In most instances, the public key is used to actually encrypt the plaintext into the ciphertext, and the private key is used to decrypt the ciphertext back into a more decipherable format that is comprehensible and easy to understand.

Thus in this regard, it is the sending party that uses the public key and the receiving party that uses the private key. Because of this, the asymmetric cryptography approach offers much more layers of security than when compared to the symmetric cryptography approach. But the primary disadvantage here is that by using two separate keys, this process requires much computational and processing power.

Asymmetric cryptography is also known as "public key cryptography," and it can be defined as:

> Public-key cryptography, or asymmetric cryptography, is an encryption scheme that uses two mathematically related, but not identical, keys – a public key and a private key. Unlike symmetric key algorithms that rely on one key to both encrypt and decrypt, each key performs a unique function. The public key is used to encrypt and the private key is used to decrypt.
>
> It is computationally infeasible to compute the private key based on the public key. Because of this, public keys can be freely shared, allowing users an easy and convenient method for encrypting content and verifying digital signatures, and private keys can be kept secret, ensuring only the owners of the private keys can decrypt content and create digital signatures.[4]

Here some of the other key advantages of public key cryptography:

1. Key Establishment:
   Numerous cryptographic algorithms can be used in this regard, such as the Diffie-Hellman Key Exchange (DHKE) and the RSA Key Transport Protocols. These algorithms are very robust in nature, and are used quite often in this kind of infrastructure.
2. Nonrepudiation:
   Using asymmetric cryptography (or public key cryptography) provides very strong levels of ciphertext integrity by using the previously mentioned algorithms.
3. Identification:
   The authenticity of both the sending and receiving parties can be confirmed easily by making use of a challenge–response system along with digital signatures.

However, in order to fully ensure that the asymmetric cryptography approach is running at optimal levels, a "hybrid protocol" technique is utilized.

This is where other security protocols are used in conjunction with the earlier mentioned protocols as well, such as SSL/TLS and IPSec, as reviewed extensively in Chapter 1.

It should be noted that another disadvantage of asymmetric cryptography is that it requires the use of very long keys. While this affords very strong layers of protection, such long keys can actually greatly slow down both the encryption and the decryption processes. Apart from the two cryptographic algorithms just described, there are other important cryptographic algorithms that need to be reviewed as well, as follows:

1. Algorithms based on integer factorization schemes:
   The basic premise behind this is that it is very difficult to factor large integers. An example of this is the RSA algorithm, as discussed previously.
2. Algorithms based on discrete logarithm schemes:
   This is based upon using finite fields. Examples of this include the DHKE and the digital signature algorithm (DSA).
3. Algorithms based on elliptic curve schemes:
   This is actually a subset of the previous item, and typical examples of this include the elliptic curve Diffie-Hellman Key Exchange (ECDH) and the elliptic curve digital signature algorithm (ECDSA).

Each of these can be used to further enhance the mechanisms of the public key and private key establishment and provide nonrepudiation via the use of digital signatures. The following table depicts the recommended bit key lengths for all of the asymmetric cryptography algorithms just discussed[3]:

Algorithm	Cryptosystem	80 Bits	128 Bits	192 Bits	256 Bits
Integer Factorization	RSA	1024 bit	3072 bit	7680 bit	15630 bit
Discrete Logarithm	DH, DSA, Elgamal	1024 bit	3072 bit	7680 bit	15360 bit
Elliptic Curves	ECDH, ECDSA	160 bit	256 bit	384 bit	512 bit
Symmetric Key	AES, 3DES	80 bit	128 bit	192 bit	256 bit

Based upon this table, the complexity of these algorithms will expand the corresponding cube bit length. With the RSA algorithm, if the bit length is increased from 1024 bits to 3076 bits, this will result in a processing speed that is 3^3 (which equals 27) slower than normal. As one can see, this can cause a huge constraint on both the web application and the server that it resides upon.

The Mathematics behind Asymmetric Cryptography

In order to fully grasp the fundamentals behind the algorithms, it is important to present an overview of the mathematics that drives them, which is reviewed in this subsection. They are as follows:

- The Euclidean algorithm
- The extended Euclidean algorithm
- The Euler Phi function
- Fermat's little theorem
    1. The Euclidean Algorithm:
        This algorithm first starts by calculating what is known as the greatest common divisor (GCD). It is represented by the following formula:

        $$GCD \ (Ro, \ R1)$$

        where Ro and R1 are positive integers.

        But keep in mind that very large integers are used in asymmetric cryptography, and using the factoring just shown will not work efficiently. It will take much more computational and processing power to use this kind of approach. Instead, another type of algorithm is needed, which is known as the Euclidean algorithm. This assumes that Ro>R1 and that both integers are positive. The Euclidean algorithm is represented as follows:

        $$GCD(Ro\text{-}R1, \ R1) = GCD[g^*(x,y), \ (g^*y)] = g$$

        What is derived from this is that the issue of finding the GCD of any two large integers to the GCD of two much smaller integers can be accomplished by making use of a recursive process, which is as follows:

        $$GCD(R0,R1) = GCD(R1,0) = Ri$$

        It is important to note that the Euclidean algorithm will automatically terminate in an asymmetric cryptography approach if the remainder value is in the state of $Ri = 0$. Because of this, the Euclidean algorithm has been deemed as an efficient one to use, even with very large integers. The number of computational iterations that are needed is equal to the number of inputs that are needed. So, for example, if the number of required iterations is equal to 1024, then 1024 * constant value is required.
    2. The Extended Euclidean Algorithm:
        The goal of the extended Euclidean algorithm is to quickly compute modular inverses, as this is an essential for public key cryptography–based systems. The extended Euclidean algorithm is represented as follows:

        $$GCD(Ro,R1) = s^*Ro + t^*R1$$

where the variables "s" and "t" represent the integer coefficients. This is also often referred to as the Diophantine equation. In turn, the variables "s" and "t" are computed by the following mathematical formula:

$$Ri = GCD(Ro, R1) = SiRo + T1R1 = SRo + TR1$$

3. The Euler Phi Function:
   An important property that is used in the RSA algorithm (which is the focal point of the next section) is the Euler Phi function. It is mathematically represented as follows:

$$0/(M)$$

The value "M" is calculated by factorization, which is represented as follows:

$$M = P1\wedge e1, P2\wedge e2, \ldots Pn\wedge en$$

Given this, $0/(M)$ can be calculated as follows:

$$0/(M) = Pi\wedge ei - Pi\wedge ei - 1$$

This factorization process is very important for the RSA algorithm, which facilitates the decryption of the ciphertext.

4. Fermat's Little Theorem:
   This algorithm can be used to check the efficiency of a public key cryptography infrastructure. It is represented as follows:

$$A\wedge p - 1 = 1 (\mod p)$$

where "A" is calculated as follows:

$$A\wedge P = a (\mod p)$$

This theorem can be further extended into what is known as Euler's theorem, which is mathematically described as follows:

$$A\wedge 0/(M) = 1 (\mod m)$$

The RSA Algorithm

The RSA algorithm is deemed to be one of the most crucial algorithms that is used in asymmetric (or public key) cryptography. Because of this this, it has been widely deployed across many web applications and the servers that they reside upon, primarily because of the robust security features that it possesses. It is used primarily to encrypt data while it is transit (for example, from the device of the end user to the web application server and vice versa) and for creating digital signature.

It is important to note at this point that the RSA algorithm has not been designed to replace symmetric-based ciphers; rather, its main purpose is to make use of its specialized encryption functionality for creating key exchanges in conjunction with a symmetric-based cipher.

In this particular instance, the RSA algorithm is often used in association with the AES algorithm, because of its symmetric-based cipher functionalities. The mathematical premise behind the RSA algorithm is integer factorization. For example, multiplying two very large prime numbers and obtaining its product is quite easy to compute. But factoring this product is very difficult to do, which gives the RSA algorithm one of its key strengths. In fact, Euler's theorem and Euler's Phi function (which were reviewed in the last subsection) are also quite heavily used with the RSA algorithm. The encryption process in the RSA algorithm is mathematically represented as follows:

$$Y = Ekpub^{\wedge}x = x^{\wedge}e \bmod n$$

where:

   Kpub = the public key (n, e)

   X = the plaintext

The decryption process in the RSA algorithm is mathematically represented as follows:

$$X = Dkpr^{\wedge}y = y^{\wedge}d \bmod n$$

where:

   Kpr = the private key (d)

   Y = the ciphertext

It should be noted at this point that x, y, n, and d are extremely large numbers, about 1024 bits in total length, and even larger. The variable "e" is also referred to as the encryption or public exponent, and the variable "d" is also referred to as the decryption or private exponent. Further, the general requirements for the RSA algorithm are as follows:

■ Since a cyberattacker potentially has access to the public key, the private key cannot be computed given the values of "e" and "n."
■ One cannot encrypt more than "l" bits of ciphertext in the cases where "l" is greater than the specified bit length of "n."

- x^e mod n must be easy to calculate for the purposes of encryption, as well as y^d mod n for the purposes of decryption
- For any given value of "n," there should be many more public key and private key pairs in order to avoid what is known as a brute-force attack.

A very unique feature of most asymmetric (public key) cryptography approaches is that there is first an initial phase where the public keys and the private keys are first computed. This can prove to be quite a complex process if stream-based ciphers are not used. With respect to the RSA algorithm, this is how this process is initiated:

- First, two extremely large integers are chosen, denoted by the variables of "p" and "q."
- Second, the computation where n = p*q is done,.
- Third, 0/(n) is computed by (p-1)*(q-1).
- Fourth, the public exponent "e" is calculated, where e = [1, 2 ... . O/(n) -1] so that the GCD can be computed as follows:

$$GCD[e, O/(n)] = 1$$

- Fifth, the private key is calculated as follows:

$$D*e = 1 \bmod 0/(n)$$

The Use of Fast Exponentiation in the RSA Algorithm

As was stated previously, the RSA algorithm is based upon those mathematics that contain very large integers. The result is that this can take an enormous amount of both computational and processing power. In the last subsection, we demonstrated the encryption and decryption formulae that are used in the RSA algorithm. These can actually be combined in order to product a faster means by which to further process the very large integers.

This is mathematically represented as follows:

$$X \rightarrow {}^\wedge SQ, X^2 \rightarrow MUL, X^3 \rightarrow MUL, X^4 \rightarrow MUL, X^5, ...$$

where:

SQ = the Squaring Component

MUL = the Multiplication Component

The values for the exponents noted in this equation are typically chosen in the bit range of 1024 to 3072, and where it is needed, even larger than this. This is also known as the square and multiple algorithm. One of the key advantages to this approach is that it provides the means in which to perform both the squaring and the multiplicative functions of "x" by computing "x^H."

Also, this algorithm works by literally examining the exponential bit from the left to the right. In each and every iteration, the result that is yielded is ultimately squared. But this exponent that has been examined must contain a numerical value of at least 1. This is the only instance where the current result is multiplied "x" following any *squaring* computations that may have transpired earlier.

The Use of Fast Encryption with Shorter Public Key Exponentiation

This is another technique that can be used with the RSA algorithm, and it is represented by the following matrix[3]:

Public Key "e"	"e" as a Binary String	#MUL + #SQ
3	11(2)	2
17	10002(2)	5
2^16 + 1	1000000000000000(2)	17

It is important to note at this point that the use of short public key exponentiation from within the RSA algorithm is considered to be mathematically a very fast process, which requires an even lesser amount of computational and processing power than the technique just reviewed. But even with this newer technique, the RSA algorithm could still theoretically slow down if the private key with a value of "d" is utilized for decryption purposes.

The Chinese Remainder Theorem (CRT)

This theorem allows for a moderate acceleration of the RSA algorithm when the value of "d" is used, as described in the last subsection. The basic goal here is to break up any long mathematical computations into two different processes into what are known as modulo exponentiations. This is done in a three-step fashion, as demonstrated next:

1. The Transformation of an Input Value:
   The goal here is to minimize the base element "x modulo" into two different factors, known as "p" and "q," respectively. The result of this is called the modular representation of "x":

$$Xp = x \bmod p$$
$$Xq = x \bmod q$$

2. The Exponentiation into the CRT Domain:
With the last step accomplished, the following exponentiations can now be done:

$$Yp = Xp^\wedge dp \bmod p$$
$$Yq = Xq^\wedge dq \bmod q$$

The following new exponential values are calculated by the following formulae:

$$Dp = d \bmod (p\text{-}1)$$
$$Dq = d \bmod (q\text{-}1)$$

Once this has been done, the values of "Dp" and "Dq" are now bounded with other values of "p" and "q." This is also true of the values of "Yp" and "Yq."
3. The Inverse Transformation
The very last step to be done is taking the values of "Yp" and "Yq" and converting them into a modular-like expression. This is mathematically done as:

$$Y = [QCp]Yp + [P^\wedge Cq]yq \bmod n$$

where Cp is computed as $q^\wedge\text{-}1 \bmod p$ and Cq is computed as $p^\wedge\text{-}1 \bmod q$.

The end result of these three steps is that the overall speed of the RSA algorithm has now increased by a factor of 4×. This not only provides a more robust level of security for the web application, but it can also speed up the encryption process, especially when PII is submitted into the web application by the end user.

How to Find Large Prime Integers for the RSA Algorithm

So far, we have addressed that when using the RSA algorithm, very large prime integers are used. But one item that has not been addressed yet is how these numbers are selected, or even generated. In other words, how do we obtain the specific values for "p" and "q," respectively? This issue will be addressed in this subsection.

Keep in mind that the product of an RSA algorithm modulus is mathematically defined as follows:

$$N = p^*q$$

The prime numbers that are used in this calculation must contain half of the bit length of "N." For instance, if we assign the bit value of 1024 to "N," then the values of "p" and "q" should each be about 512 bits in length. In order to pick any large prime number, the general approach is to generate these integers at random, which is done by a tool known as the random number generator (RNG). The RNG must be nonpredictable in nature, because if a cyberattacker can guess one of these two large prime numbers, the RSA algorithm can then be broken into quite easily. Further, two questions must also be answered:

- How many random integers need to be generated and tested before it is determined that an integer is actually prime or not?
- How quickly can be this process actually be achieved?

The answer to the first question is actually dependent upon the probability laws of statistics. In this case, the prime number theory is used, which is mathematically defined as follows:

$$P = 2/\ln(p)$$

where P is a prime number.

The answer to the second question – which two types of mathematical tests are used – is:

- The Fermat primality test
- The Miller-Rabin primality test
  1. The Fermat Primality Test:
     This type of test is actually based upon Fermat's little theorem. In terms of a programming source code, it can be represented as follows:

```
FOR i = 1 TO x
Choose random a>= (2, 3, . . . .p-2)
IF a^p-1 =/1
RETURN ("p is a composite number")
RETURN ("p is likely prime")
```

One of the advantages of this kind of test is that it can be used for all large prime numbers that need to be tested. For example, if a^p-1 =/1, then it is deemed not to be a prime number. But the disadvantage is that this process cannot work in the reverse fashion. In other words, there could be other numbers that are not detected which could be very well be

prime. Technically, these are also referred to as Carmichael numbers in the world of cryptography.
2. The Miller-Rabin Primality Test:
   This is actually deemed to be much more efficient than the Fermat primality test. Once again, in terms of a programming source code, it can be represented as follows:

```
FOR i=1 TO s
Choose random a>= (2, 3, ....p-2)
Z=a^r mod p
IF z=/1 and z=/p-1
FOR j=1 TO u-1
Z=z^2 mod p
IF z=1
RETURN ("p is a composite number")
IF Z=/p-1
RETURN ("p is a composite number")
RETURN ("p is likely a prime number")
```

The Use of Padding in the RSA Algorithm

Although the RSA algorithm is a very robust and powerful tool be used in an asymmetric (public key) cryptography infrastructure, it does suffer from a number of shortcomings, which are as follows:

1. It is deterministic in nature:
   A specific piece of plaintext message is always attached to a specific piece of associated ciphertext. If the same private key is used, it is likely that the cyberattacker will be able to derive certain relationships between the plaintext and the ciphertext, and from there, launch the cyberattack.
2. The inverse numerical values:
   In this instance, if the plaintext values are x=0, x=1, x=2, etc., the same inverse will hold true of the ciphertext: x=0, x=−1, x=−2, etc.
3. Small values:
   If, for some reason, small numerical values are used in the RSA algorithm, it could prove vulnerable to a cyberattack. Thus, that is why very large prime integers are used for this very reason.
4. Malleability:
   This occurs when a cyberattacker can take a ciphertext, transform it into another variant of a ciphertext, and from there convert it into a plaintext. Mathematically, this is represented as:

$$(s^e y)^d = s^{ed} x^{ed} = s\ x\ mod\ n$$

A solution to this is to use a technique called padding. This is where a random structure is introduced into the plaintext before it is converted into the ciphertext. It is accomplished in the following steps:

1. A string is generated of a length determined by the following formula:

$$K - |M| - 2|H| - 2$$

2. Concatenation then occurs, where a single byte is created with a known hexadecimal value of 0×01, and a data block, known as "DB," is created of a length k - |H| -1 bytes. This is represented as:

$$DB = HASH(L)\|PS\|0x01\|M$$

3. A random-byte string is then generated of length |H|.
4. The variable "dbMASK" is calculated as follows:

$$dbMASK = MGF\ (seed,\ k - |H| - 1)$$

where MGF is the Masked Generation Function.
5. maskedDB = DB O/db MASK
6. seedMASK = MGF (maskedDB, |H|)
7. maskedSeed = seed)/seedMASK
8. Finally, a concatenation occurs where the hexadecimal value of 0×00, maskedSeed, and maskedDB is used to create a ciphertext message of "k" bytes in length, using the following formula:

$$EM = 0\ x\ 00\|maskedSeed\|maskedDB$$

Specific Cyberattacks on the RSA Algorithm

The RSA algorithm is prone to three types of cyberattacks:

■ Protocol attacks
■ Mathematical attacks
■ Side-channel attacks
  1. Protocol Attacks:
     These kinds of cyberattacks exploit both the known and the unknown vulnerabilities that are in the RSA algorithm. In this regard, the most common threat vehicles are those that target its malleability. But the concept of padding (reviewed in the last subsection) can be used to help mitigate the risk of this kind of cyberattack from happening.

2. Mathematical Attacks:

    The main type of cyberattack that occurs here is when the factoring process is not computed properly, in which the value of 0/(n) can be calculated easily the cyberattacker. It can be done in the following three-step mathematical process:

$$0/(n) = (p-1)*(q-1)$$
$$D^\wedge-1 = e \bmod 0/(n)$$
$$X = y^\wedge d \bmod n$$

    In order to avoid this kind of cyberattack, the value of the modulus must contain a very large integer. An ideal value here is at least 1024 bits or higher, typically in the range of 2048 bits to 4096 bits.

3. Side-Channel Attacks:

    These types of cyberattacks further exploit the weaknesses and the vulnerabilities that are found in the private key. This is typically accomplished using physical-based channels in the asymmetric (public key cryptography) infrastructure. One mathematical method that is used to avoid this is to execute a multiplication with various kinds of dummy variables that are associated with an exponent bit value of "0."

The Digital Signature Algorithm

The digital signature algorithm (DSA) is actually an algorithm that was established by the U.S. federal government and was designed exclusively for the use of digital signatures. The concept of the DSA was first proposed by the National Institute of Standards and Technology (NIST). It also has certain advantages, in that the signature is only a mere 320 bits long. But for the purposes of this section, the DSA will be used in a format that is 1024 bits long.

Both the public key and the private key are generated by the following process:

1. A prime number, known as "p," is generated where $2^\wedge 1023 < p < 2^\wedge 1024$.
2. A prime divisor, known as "q," is then found of p-1 where $2^\wedge 159 < q < 2^\wedge 160$.
3. An element "A" is then found where ORD(A) = q.
4. A random number of "d" is then selected where 0 < d < q.
5. A value known as "B" is then calculated where A^d mod p.
6. The generated public key and private key are now as follows:

$$Kpub = (p, q, A, B)$$
$$Kpr = (d)$$

The basis of the DSA is that two cyclical mathematical groups are involved. One of these is the larger group that is represented as "Zp^0/," which has a total length of 1024 bits. The second grouping is actually a subset of "Zp^0/," which is 160 bits long.

Digital Signature Computation and Verification Process for the DSA

In this process, the DSA consists of two distinct digital signatures, known as "r" and "s." They are only 160 bits long, and thus, the total length is 320 bits. The two digital signatures are computed in the following process:

1. A random integer is chosen as an ephemeral key, known as "Ke" where $0 < Ke < q$.
2. A value of "R" is computed with following formula:

$$(A^{\wedge}ke \bmod p)$$

3. A value of "S" is computed with following formula:

$$[SHA(x) + d * r]Ke^{\wedge}\text{-1} \bmod q$$

The two digital signatures, once computed in the earlier process, are then completely verified by making use of this methodology:

1. An auxiliary value of "W" is then computed with the following:

$$W = S^{\wedge}\text{-1} \bmod q$$

2. An auxiliary value of "U1" is then computed with the following:

$$U1 = w*SHA(x) \bmod q$$

3. An auxiliary value of "U1" is then computed with the following:

$$U2 = w*r \bmod q$$

4. Finally, a value known as "V" is calculated as follows:

$$(A^{\wedge}n*B^{\wedge}U2 \bmod p) \bmod q$$

5. The following mathematical proof is then used to confirm or reject the validity of the digital signatures:

$$V = r \bmod q \rightarrow \text{This is a valid digital signature}$$

$$V = /r \bmod q \rightarrow \text{This is an invalid digital signature}$$

The Prime Number Generation Process in the DSA

These particular numbers, as used by the DSA, are generated by the following source code process:

```
Find a prime number denoted as "q" where 2^150 < q < 2^160
FOR i=1 to 4096
Generate a random integer known as "M" with 2^2013 < M <
2^1024
Mr=M mod 2q
p-1 = M-M1
If the value "p" is prime
RETURN (p,q)
I=i+1
GOTO the first step
```

Security Issues with the DSA

Just like all of the other cryptographic algorithms covered thus far in this chapter, the DSA is also prone to being hacked. For example, the cyberattacker could quite possibly calculate the private key by using the following discrete logarithmic formula:

$$D = \log aB \bmod p$$

There are two distinct ways this could happen:

■ The index calculus attack
■ Subgroup exploitation
  1. The Index Calculus Attack:
     In order for this to happen, the value of "p" must be at least 1024 bits long. In order to avoid this, it is highly recommended that bit lengths between 2048 and 3072 be used.
  2. Subgroup Exploitation:
     This situation arises where the value of "A" only generates a very small subgroup, which has a bit size of 2^{2014}.

Finally, in order to help mitigate these two types of cyberattacks, the NIST recommends the following bit lengths for the DSA[3]:

The Value of "p"	The Value of "q"	Hash Output Value	Security Level Value
1024	160	160	80
2048	224	224	112
3072	256	256	128

It should be noted that the 1024-bit length provides a reasonable layer of security, whereas the 2048- and the 3072-bit lengths provide the maximum level of protection for the DSA. Also, when it comes to using the DSA, a new pair of a randomly generated public key and private key must be used each and every time.

The Elliptic Curve Digital Signature Algorithm

This algorithm possesses a number of key advantages over the other algorithms reviewed in this chapter, namely that of the RSA algorithm and the DSA algorithm. These are as follows:

- The bit lengths for the ECDSA algorithm are typically in the range of 160 to 256 bits; this is the equivalent to the 1024 to 3072 bits in the RSA algorithm. Thus, much stronger levels of security are provided.
- Because of these shorter bits, the ECDSA algorithm results in greatly reduced processing times, as well as the need for computational resources.

The Generation of the Public Key and the Private Key Using the ECDSA Algorithm

The mathematical framework is actually embedded in the prime number field known as "Zp" and the Galois field represented as "GF (2^m)." The Galois field was reviewed in detail earlier in this chapter. The process for generating both the public key and the private key is as follows:

1. An elliptic curve known as "E" is constructed with the following parameters:
   - A modulus P
   - Prime number coefficients known as "a" and "b"
   - A prime number point known as "A," which creates a cyclical group of prime number orders known as "q"

2. A random number integer known as "d" is created with $0 < d < q$.
3. Finally, the computation where B=dA is then accomplished.

Through this process, the public key and private key are now created, which are as follows, respectively:

$$Kpub = (p, a, b, q, A, B)$$
$$Kpr = (d)$$

The public key and private key will thus be 160 bits, which is the minimum level of security that is accepted by the ECDSA algorithm.

The Signature and the Verification Process of the ECDSA Algorithm

For the public/private key to be 160 bits, the ECDSA algorithm consists of a pair of prime integers, known as "r" and "s," represented as (r, s). It should be noted that these prime integers have the same bit length of the value "q" (as reviewed in the last subsection). Because of this, the digital signatures that are created for the ECDSA algorithm are also fairly compact and light in nature.

The digital signature generation process is as follows:

1. A random integer is selected by making use of an ephemeral key, which is known as "Ke." This is then created with $0 < Ke < q$.
2. The value "R" is computed using KeA.
3. The parameter of r=xR is then set.
4. Finally, the last computation is as follows:

$$S = [h(x) + d * r)kE^{-1} \bmod q$$

The digital signature verification process is as follows:

1. An auxiliary value of "w" is computed as:

$$W = s^{-1} \bmod q$$

2. An auxiliary value of "u1" is computed as:

$$U1 = w * h(x) \bmod q$$

3. An auxiliary value of "u2" is computed as:

$$U2 = w * r \bmod q$$

4. The value "P" is computed as:

$$P = u1A + u2B$$

5. The verification of the digital signature known as "VERKpub [x, (r, s)] comes from the following rule set:

Xp = r mod q → This is a *valid* digital signature.

Xp = /r mod q → This is *not a valid* digital signature.

The following matrix shows the recommended bit lengths for the ECDSA algorithm, as well as its level of security[3]:

The Value of "q"	The Hash Output	The Security Level
192 bits	192 bits	96 bits
224 bits	224 bits	112 bits
256 bits	256 bits	128 bits
384 bits	384 bits	192 bits
512 bits	512 bits	256 bits

The Use of Hash Functions

Throughout this entire chapter, we have reviewed at length the usage of digital signatures. But there are certain limitations to it. For example, when it is used in conjunction with the RSA algorithm, the plaintext message that is being encrypted cannot be any longer than the length of the modulus. In other words, the plaintext cannot be any longer than 128–384 bytes long. Most of the web applications that are developed and implemented today transmit information and data that are much longer than that.

One theoretical solution to this is to divide the plaintext message, denoted as "x," into separate blocks known as "x1." From here, separate digital signatures could then be created. But there are three fundamental problems with this approach, which are as follows:

1. A much higher computational load:
   Even though separate blocks are created and are much smaller in size, this will still place a huge workload upon the web application server. The primary reason for this is that these smaller blocks are subsequently aggregated together to form one large block, which consists of a huge byte size.
2. A large message overhead:
   The plaintext message is actually doubled in size because it also contains the digital signature that must be verified by the receiver of the message.

3. Various security vulnerabilities:
   This can occur when the cyberattacker when gets a hold of the plaintext message and can remove the digital signatures that are associated with it. Or the plaintext messages could be covertly rearranged, or even reassembled with malicious plaintext messages.

Because of these limitations, the best solution is to create just one short digital signature of any length that is possible. This is where hashing comes into play. It can be specifically defined as follows:

Hashing is the transformation of a string of characters into a usually shorter fixed-length value or key that represents the original string. Hashing is used to index and retrieve items in a database because it is faster to find the item using the shorter hashed key than to find it using the original value. It is also used in many encryption algorithms.[5]

Some important characteristics of hashing include the following:

■ It should be applied to a plaintext message of any size
■ It should be fast to compute.
■ The output should consist of a fixed length, which is completely independent of the input length. The desirable output length of a hashing function should be in the range of 128–512 bits.

The Security Requirements of Hash Functions

It is important to note at this point that hash functions do not actually possess any public keys or private keys by themselves. Therefore, there are three important security properties that a hash function must have, as follows:

■ Preimage resistance
■ Another type of preimage resistance
■ Collision resistance
   1. Preimage Resistance:
      This is very often referred to as one-wayness. This procedure is computed as follows:

$$[Ek(x), sigKpr, B^{\wedge}(Z)]$$

where Ek () = the symmetric cipher.
      The digital signature and its corresponding hash function are calculated as follows:

$$S = SIGKpr, b^{\wedge}(Z) = z^{\wedge}d \bmod n$$

At this point, if the hash function is not one-way in nature, the plaintext message can be very easily computed by the cyberattacker. But if it is one-way, the plaintext message cannot be reassembled again after it has been encrypted.

2. Another Type of Preimage Resistance:

This is also referred to as weak collision resistance. In other words, if two digital signatures are present, it is imperative that the corresponding plaintext messages do not compute to the same hash function value. In terms of mathematics, the two unique plaintext messages should be where X1=/X2 and should also not possess equal hash function values where:

$$Z1 = h(x^\wedge 1) = h(x^\wedge 2) = Z2$$

The theory for this lies in what is known as the "pigeonhole principle." This is where it is assumed if you own 100 pigeons, but in the pigeon cage there are only 99 holes present, one hole will have two pigeon occupants in it. As it relates to hash functions, each one has a bit length that is fixed. As a result, there are only two possible output values. Because of this, the total number of inputs to the hash function is theoretically infinite, and it is quite possible that any of these inputs could be calculated to the same output value. In order to prevent this from happening, the hash function should be created in such a way that given X1 and h(X2), it would be theoretically impossible to create X2 in a way that h(X1) = h(X2).

3. Collision Resistance:

A hash function is deemed to be "collision resistant" or have strong levels of it if two different input values cannot be computed, where X1 =/X2 with h(X1) = h(X2). One of the primary theories that drive this requirement is known in the world of statistics as the "birthday paradox." For example, how many individuals are needed at a given event so that there is a reasonable level of probability that at least two of them will have the same birthdate? The first approach to this problem is to examine it from what is known as a piecewise approach. To determine this for two people, the following statistical formula is used:

$$P(\text{no collision among 2 people}) = (1\text{-}1/365)$$

To determine this for three people, the following statistical formula is used:

$$P(\text{no collision among 3 people}) = (1\text{-}1/365) * (1\text{-}2/365)$$

To determine this for an "x" number of people, the following statistical formula is used:

P(no collision among "t" people) = (1-1/365) * (1-2/365)...[1-(r-1)/365]

As it turns out, from these computations, it only takes about 23 people to have at least a 50% chance of two of them having the same birthdate. It is calculated as follows:

> P(at least one collision) = 1-P(no collision) =
> 1-(1-1/365)...[1-(23-1/365)] =
> 0.507 or about 50%

Given this example of the birthday paradox, the statistical probability for a hash function to consist of no values is calculated as follows:

P(no collision) = [1-(1/2^n)]*[1-(2/2^n)]...[1-(t-1/2^n)]

But to calculate the statistical relationship among the total number of hash functions that are needed as a function of the ciphertext output length of "n," the following formula is utilized:

$$T = 2^{(n+1)/2} * SQUARE\ ROOT[\ln(1/1-Y)]$$

Probably the most important takeaway from the birthday paradox as it relates to the hash function is that the number of ciphertext messages that need the use of a hash function is approximately equal to the square root of the total number of output values that are possible. This is mathematically represented as:

$$SQUARE\ ROOT\ 2^n = 2^{n/2}$$

It is also important to note that the typical output length for a hash function is 128 bits, if not longer. The following matrix depicts the various hash function output values in order to avoid any sort of collision:

Hash Output Lengths

A	128 Bit	160 Bit	256 Bit	384 Bit	512 Bit
0.5	2^65	2^81	2^129	2^193	2^257
0.9	2^67	2^82	2^130	2^194	2^258

A Technical Overview of Hash Function Algorithms

There are two basic types of hash functions:

■ The Dedicated Hash Function: These are specific mathematical algorithms that are designed to serve exclusively hash functions.
■ Block Cipher–Based Hash Functions: These are block ciphers that are used to create hash functions.

An important concept that should be noted here at this point is the Merkle-Damgård construction. This is when a hash function process an "x" length of ciphertext, and from there, creates a fixed-length output. This is very often done by segmenting the input into a sequence of blocks that are of equal size and are processed sequentially. In this scenario, the value of the hash function can be thought of as the last iteration of a compression function.

1. The Dedicated Hash Function:
   It should be noted that dedicated hash functions are actually customized in order to specifically meet the needs of the web application in question. There are numerous hash functions in this grouping, which include the following:
   – The MD4 family
   – The MD5
   – The SHA family
   – RIPEMD
   The MD4 is actually a message digest hash function and was developed by Ron Rivest. It makes use of 32-bit variables, and all of the functionalities that are carried out make use of the statistical properties of XOR, AND, OR, and other types of data negation. The MD5 is a further enhanced version of the MD4. It makes use of a 128-bit output, and the collision resistance (as reviewed in the last subsections) is about 2^{65}.

   The MD5 is heavily used by web applications and the servers that they reside upon. For instance, it can be used for calculating various checksums of the files that make up the web application or for even permanently storing any hash functions that are used, either by IT staff that is administering the web application or the end user that is accessing it.

   Because of this, the NIST developed a brand-new hash function, which was known as the Secure Hash Algorithm (SHA). The first version of this is known as SHA-O, and the second version is known as SHA-1. The primary difference between these two resides in the compression functions that are used to further the levels of security for these hash functions.

   The output of both the SHA-0 and the SHA-1 are at 160 bits. The SHA-1 hash function is also used extensively by web applications. The collision resistance of both of these hash functions is rated at 2^{80}; thus, they should not be used with some of the other encryption algorithms, most notably the AES algorithm, as reviewed earlier in this chapter. The primary reason for this is that this specific algorithm has a security level in the range of 128 to 256 bits.

The NIST also came out with three more versions of the SHA-1, and these are as follows:

- SHA-256
- SHA-384
- SHA-512

Their hash function digest bits are 256, 384, and 512, respectively. These, including that of the SHA-1, are grouped into another family known as SHA-2. The following matrix illustrates the main parameters of all of these hash functions just described[3]:

Algorithm	Output	Input	# of Rounds	Collisions Detected
MD5	128 bits	512 bits	64	Yes
SHA-1	160 bits	512 bits	80	None detected
SHA-224	224 bits	512 bits	64	None detected
SHA-256	256 bits	512 bits	64	None detected
SHA-384	384 bits	1024 bits	80	None detected
SHA-512	512 bits	1024 bits	80	None detected

Block Cipher–Based Hash Functions

Hash functions can also be created by making use of block cipher chaining techniques. In these particular instances, a ciphertext message, denoted as "x," can be divided into further blocks known as "Xi," which are of a fixed size. The latter are encrypted into a block cipher known as "e," which has a block size known as "b." After "Xi" is encrypted, a statistical-based XOR value is thus calculated, which is then associated with the block of the original ciphertext message. The last output value is calculated as follows:

$$X1, x2, \ldots. Xn \text{ where } Hn = H(x)$$

One of the techniques that are used to create the block from the ciphertext message is mathematically demonstrated as follows:

$$Hi = Eg\ (Hi\text{-}1)^\wedge[(Xi)0/Xi]$$

This is known as the Matyas-Meyer-Oseas hash function. There are other techniques as well, which are as follows:

■ The Davies-Meyer Hash Function:

$$Hi = Hi\text{-}1\ 0/EXi(Hi\text{-}1)$$

■ The Miyaguchi-Preneel Hash Function:

$$Hi = Hi\text{-}1\ 0/Xi\ 0/Eg(Hi\text{-}1)\wedge(Xi)$$

All of these hash function techniques just described need to have initial values that are assigned to the variable "Ho." The commonality between all of these hash functions is that their bit size is equivalent to the block width of the ciphertext that it is associated with. These techniques can also be used to create even larger hash function message digests, which produce a block length of "b," which is twice the size of other blocks that are created from the ciphertext.

In this instance just described, the "Hirose construction" technique can be used. This consists of a 128-bit hash function output and a divided block size of 64 bits.

Technical Details of the Secure Hash Algorithm SHA-1

As was described in the last subsection, SHA-1 is the most used hash function digest that is utilized in the MD4 grouping. Its mathematical compression functionality in many ways operates like a block cipher. In this particular instance, the required input bit is based upon the previous hash function value of Hi-1, and the output is calculated by "Xi." This value is 160 bits at minimum, and can even go as high as $2\wedge64$ bits.

During its mathematical compression cycle, the ciphertext message is processed in 512-bit pieces. This specific compression functionality consists of 80 rounds, which are further divided into four segments, which are 20 rounds long. In this subsection, we examine the following:

■ Preprocessing
■ The Hash computation
  1. Preprocessing:
     Preprocessing uses the concept of padding, which was described in detail earlier in this chapter. In order to process the ciphertext message in a 512-bit piece, the following computations are required:

$$K = 512 - 64 - 1 - i$$
$$= 448 - (l+1)\ mod\ 512$$

where:

X = the ciphertext message

L = the bit length (which is actually a 64 − bit binary representation)

After this has been accomplished, the 512-bit piece is then divided with the following computation, before the compression functionality is actually applied:

$$Xi = [Xi^\wedge(0) \ Xi^\wedge(1)...Xi^\wedge(15)$$

where $Xi^\wedge(k)$ = the 32-bit size.

2. The Hash Computation:

As just described, it is divided into four main segments. These are determined by the following mathematical algorithm:

$$Wj = X(j) \text{ where } 0 < j <= 15$$
$$Wj = (Wj\text{-}16^\wedge0/Wj \text{ - } 14^\wedge0/Wj\text{-}8^\wedge0/Wj\text{-}3) \text{ where } 16 <= j <= 79$$

where $X(j)$ = a circular left shift of the ciphertext message by a series of "n" positions.

The four stages are similar in composition by nature, consisting of 20 rounds. After the 80 rounds have been completed (as just described), the bit output is then added to the bit input with the following computation:

$$Hi\text{-}1 \text{ Mod } 2^\wedge32$$

It is important that in each of the 20 separate rounds a functionality is included. Statistical-based Boolean operators are used in this regard, which include the following:

− Logical AND (represented as "^")
− Logical OR (represented as "an inverse ^")
− NOT
− XOR statements

These rounds are also referred to as generalized Feistel networks.

The following matrix demonstrates the various properties of each of the four stages and their associated rounds[3]:

Stage	Round	Constant Ki	Function Fi
1	0...19	K1=5A827999	Fi(B,C,D) = (B^C)*B^D
2	20....39	K2=6ED9EBA1	F2(B,C,D)=B0/C0/D
3	40....59	K3=8F1BBCDC	F3(B,C,D) = (B^C)*(B^D)*(C*D)
4	60....79	K4=CA62C1D6	F4(B,C,D)=B0/C0/D

Key Distribution Centers

When it comes to the world of symmetric cryptography, one of the key components is the KDC. This is entirely embedded into the server, which all of the end users entrust for the distribution of the private keys in order to decrypt the ciphertext messages. Technically, this private key is also known as the key encryption key (KEK). It is also used to secure the transmission of the ciphertext that is sent from the sender to the receiver (for example, the web application server would the sender and the end user of the web application would be the receiver).

A unique feature of the KDC is that each end user that is assigned to it has a unique KEK, which is distributed via a secure means of connection once it is requested for decryption purposes. In order to accomplish this task, the KDC creates two sets of ciphertext messages known as "Ya" and "Yb." Mathematically, this is represented as follows:

$$Ya = Eka\verb|^|(Kses)$$
$$Yb = Ckb\verb|^|(Kses)$$

It is important to note that the two ciphertext messages are both further encrypted with the KEKs. Both of them can be considered "long-term" keys, meaning that their structure and integrity never change; they always remain static in nature. This is what forms the secret lines of communication between the sender and the receiver (or, for example, the web application server and the end user).

A number of security issues are associated with KDCs, which are as follows:

■ The replay attack
■ The key confirmation attack
■ Communications requirements
■ A single point of failure
■ No forward secrecy

1. The Replay Attack:
   This can happen when an old private key is reused again and it is not refreshed over a period of time. This is situation can further worsen if older private keys are used that have already been covertly compromised.
2. The Key Confirmation Attack:
   In this instance, the KDC is manipulated into thinking that a legitimate end user is requesting to establish a secure session, when it is really a cyberattacker that has initiated this.
3. Communications Requirements:
   Each and every time a new secure session is requested between the end user and the KDC, new lines of communication must be established. As a result,

this can take an enormous amount of both computational and processing power if there are many end users (say in the hundreds or even thousands) requesting a brand-new secure session.

4. A Single Point of Failure:

   One of the biggest security disadvantages of a KDC is that just one database stores all of the KEKs. If this is at all compromised, the entire KDC infrastructure will collapse.

5. No Forward Secrecy:

   This simply means that if any of the KEKs become damaged or compromised by a cyberattacker in any way, shape, or form, any further communications can be quite easily intercepted and decrypted by a malicious third party. To make matters even worse, if a certain KEK is compromised, even past communications between the sender and the receiver can be easily intercepted and decrypted. The only solution to this is to deploy a public or asymmetric cryptography infrastructure. This offers what is known as perfect forward secrecy (PFS) that alleviates the problem of both the interception and decryption of previous and future ciphertext messages.

In order to protect against replay and key confirmation attacks, a specialized protocol was developed at the Massachusetts Institute of Technology (MIT). It is called Kerberos, and it can be specifically defined as follows:

> Under Kerberos, a client (generally either a user or a service) sends a request for a ticket to the Key Distribution Center (KDC). The KDC creates a ticket-granting ticket (TGT) for the client, encrypts it using the client's password as the key, and sends the encrypted TGT back to the client. The client then attempts to decrypt the TGT, using its password. If the client successfully decrypts the TGT (i.e., if the client gave the correct password), it keeps the decrypted TGT, which indicates proof of the client's identity.
>
> The TGT, which expires at a specified time, permits the client to obtain additional tickets, which give permission for specific services. The requesting and granting of these additional tickets is user-transparent.[6]

Based on this definition, one of the primary objectives of Kerberos is to provide an enhanced means for end-user authentication. This is done primarily by establishing a sense of timeliness, with two specific methods:

- It specifies a certain lifetime, denoted with the variable "T" for the private key.
- A timestamp is also created and provided, which displays the recentness of the private key. This merely provides a sense of assurance to the receiver that the ciphertext message has not been compromised in any way.

The Public Key Infrastructure and Certificate Authority

In the last subsection, as well as throughout this entire book, we have discussed the concept of asymmetric cryptography. In this kind of infrastructure, both the public keys and private keys are used to encrypt and decrypt ciphertext messages from the web application, as well as the server it resides upon, to the end user and vice versa.

The technical name for this, as discussed, is the PKI. A PKI can be specifically defined as the following:

> Public Key Infrastructure (PKI) is the combination of software, encryption technologies, and services that enables entities to protect the security of their communications and business transactions on networks. Using a combination of private (e.g., secret) key and public key cryptography, PKI enables a number of other security services, including data confidentiality, data integrity and non-repudiation. PKI integrates digital certificates, public key cryptography, and certification authorities into one complete network security architecture.[7]

From this definition, the concept of CAs is addressed. This is at the heart of a PKI, and it can be defined as follows[8]:

> A certificate authority (CA), also sometimes referred to as a certification authority, is a company or organization that acts to validate the identities of entities (such as websites, email addresses, companies, or individual persons) and bind them to cryptographic keys through the issuance of electronic documents known as digital certificates. A digital certificate provides:
>
> ■ Authentication, by serving as a credential to validate the identity of the entity that it is issued to.
> ■ Encryption, for secure communication over insecure networks such as the Internet.
> ■ Integrity of documents signed with the certificate so that they cannot be altered by a third party in transit.

One of the most common types of certificates is the X.509 certificate. This, too, is used by many web applications and the end users that they communicate with. It consists of the following properties:

1. The Certificate Algorithm:
   This is where the type of hash function that is being used is specified. For example, this can be the SHA-1 or even the SHA-2.
2. The Issuer:
   This specifies either the entity that originally issued the digital certificate in question.

3. The Period of Validity:
   It is important to remember that the public key has a finite lifetime. The primary reason for this is that the private key that is associated with the public key could become prey for the cyberattacker.
4. The Subject:
   This includes the relevant information and data about the individuals or entities that have requested that a specific digital certificate be created.
5. The Subject's Public Key:
   This contains the relevant information and data about the public key that was created and issued. The particulars about the cryptographic algorithm that was used to create the public key are also stored here as well.

Because a PKI can be quite large and complex, with many CAs residing within them, these are also prime targets for the cyberattacker. Because of this, any public key, private key, or even digital certificate must be disabled as quickly as possible if there is any sign of trouble lurking. In order to accomplish this task, CRLs are widely deployed.

As its name implies, this is merely a listing of all of the public keys, private keys, and digital certificates that have expired, so that they cannot be used again. Even live ones can be placed on this list as well in order to render them useless in the face of a cyberattack that is occurring.

But keep in mind that CRLs are not comprehensive in nature; rather, they only contain a listing of the most recently disabled keys or certificates. This is known as a delta CRL. The primary reason for having this is that the CRL, if it was comprehensive, would be become too large to the point where it would almost be impossible to process in real time.

Resources

1 *Computer Networking: A Top Down Approach*, Kurose, J.F. & Ross, K.W., Pearson Education Group, 2008, p. 683
2 *Computer Networking: A Top Down Approach,* Kurose, J.F. & Ross, K.W., Pearson Education Group, 2008, p. 687.
3 https://www.fedidcard.gov/faq/what-pki-public-key-infrastructure-and-why-do-i-need-it
4 https://www.globalsign.com/en/ssl-information-center/what-is-public-key-cryptography/
5 https://searchsqlserver.techtarget.com/definition/hashing
6 https://web.mit.edu/kerberos/krb5-1.5/krb5-1.5.4/doc/krb5-install/What-is-Kerberos-and-How-Does-it-Work_003f.html
7 https://www.ssl.com/faqs/what-is-a-certificate-authority/
8 Paar Christof and Jan Pelzl. "Understanding Cryptography: A Textbook for Students and Practioners". 2010, Springer-Verlag Heidelberg.

Chapter 3

Penetration Testing

Introduction

"I'm just a keystroke away from downloading their entire database," said the experienced hacker! Fortunately, this was an *ethical* hacker and an expert penetration tester in my company performing an authorized test commissioned by a client, while carefully documenting the results to present to said client.

Unfortunately, there are plenty of bad actors who *would* download the "entire database" and sell or post the contents on the Dark Web or to other bad actors. Performing penetration tests is an excellent way to determine how vulnerable your systems, applications, and organizational assets are. In fact, although cybersecurity is truly multilayered and multifaceted, frequent penetration testing is a quick way to really understand what I would call infrastructural blind spots.

The intent of this chapter is to clearly define penetration testing, as well as elaborate on its requirement by multiple cyber-compliance standards and frameworks. I will also spend some time elaborating on the methodologies and elements of a thorough vs. mediocre penetration test.

Clients will often call and say, "I want a penetration test." I always make it a point to ensure we're on the same page by ascertaining whether the client wants a mere vulnerability or web app *scan*, or a proper penetration test. So how would you define the differences?

Clearly stated, a penetration test is a *real-world, simulated attack performed by certified and qualified engineers, using both automated and manual attack techniques. They professionally find and appropriately exploit all vulnerable attack vectors until they have exploited them all and professionally document all findings with clear remediation advisement, including multiple screen shots.*

Peeling the Onion

An apt description of the penetration, or "pen test," process is "peeling the onion." Vulnerability scans typically will scan just the first layer and report on findings. Though better artificial intelligence (AI) and automated processes are developing, including authenticated testing, there still is nothing like an experienced problem solver finding the first layer of vulnerabilities, exploiting them, moving to the next layer and the next, gaining system or root access, and pivoting laterally in a network to find even more opportunity. This is what I call peeling the onion.

Scans, by contrast, are fully automated, and in fact will be employed in a test much like a tool in one's auto mechanic's toolbox. The mechanic uses torque wrenches, manual and hydraulic ratchets, Phillips and flat-head screwdrivers, volt meters, and a myriad of other tools, all suited for the purpose of diagnosing and fixing your vehicle. In the same way, scanners like Nessus and Open Vas, tools like Burp Suite, Kali Linux, and dozens more are the wrenches and screwdrivers in your pen test engineer's toolkit, which, wielded with expertise, will contribute to a quality report.

True Stories

Here are some practical examples of how this process works. These true scenarios illustrate how one vulnerability or attack vector might lead to another until the compromise includes potential system takeover or admin rights of certain servers or devices.

External Testing: Auxiliary System Vulnerabilities

Our first incident is a law firm. Confidential documents. Plenty of sensitive client information. Imagine the administrator or one of the firm partners coming to work early in the morning with a full workload ahead, only to have a message appear on the screen, "This computer and all others in the firm have been encrypted. Please pay 5,000 Bitcoin to this address (bitcoin address) and the code will be given to release your machines." (Such actually happened to a company I am familiar with.)

In the case of the law firm being described, this didn't happen *but could have very easily* based on the system vulnerabilities discovered. The reason for this was a video camera system that was vulnerable. It had been installed without changing default passwords. Common brute-force tools can easily determine such passwords, thus granting system entry. In this case, the law firm was quite shocked when the engineer delivered the report with screenshots of their filing cabinets, boardroom, and other camera angles.

Such vulnerability in an auxiliary system is what led to the much-publicized breach of Target Corporation's point-of-sale (POS) systems, resulting in the exposure of 40 million credit and debit card numbers and 70 million records of personal information.[1] If a bad actor can gain access to a system, it is only a matter of time until he pivots into other systems. And that is one big factor on the side of the attacker – time. Incidentally, the auxiliary system in question here was a heating, ventilation, and air conditioning (HVAC) system.

It should be noted here that the average dwell time of a hacker, once a system has been compromised, is 180 to 416 days., depending on the research you read. That means the average attacker may have access to a system for longer than a year before they are detected.[2] In the Target case, there was plenty of time to install malware, tie into internal File Transfer Protocol (FTP) servers, and begin exfiltrating data out of the organization.

Finally, in the case of our law firm, confidentiality and integrity of the firm's private data were compromised via access to sensitive camera feeds. The two camera feeds in particular that gave access to the most confidential data were the file cabinet room and the server room. The overall risk identified to the firm as a result of the penetration test was **high**. A direct path from external attacker to sensitive corporate devices was obtained. The administrative access could be used for further compromise, such as knowing internal Internet Protocol (IP) address schemes or allowing for a physical compromise of the building undetected.

A law firm's vulnerable camera system or the HVAC system of a major corporation both point to the capacity of bad actors to do – well – bad things, as well as the critical importance of frequent penetration testing performed by an independent party that is unafraid to poke, prod, explore, and document.

Internal Testing

The next scenario involves *internal penetration testing*. Internal testing will be reviewed later but is a best practice scenario (and required for PCI, ISO 27001, NIST, and many other standards). This is where the tester is connected *behind* the firewall or is otherwise authenticated so as to view internal IP addresses. Again, due to attacker dwell times, this allows potential "showstoppers" or risky vulnerabilities to be discovered so that if an attacker *does* gain access, she won't find immediate, easy compromise of systems.

The client in question here happened to be a manufacturer with international offices. External testing had discovered minimal vulnerabilities to exploit, but the internal testing of a particular international office in the company's system was a different story.

Report Narrative

> The test engineer performed internal testing first by running enumeration scans to determine what ports and services were available. OpenVAS was also downloaded and run to look for vulnerabilities inside the reachable remote office network. Each individual port was checked to see what was listening on that port.
>
> During the research, MikroTik RouterOS devices were discovered on several servers. A few of them were vulnerable to the MikroTik "By The Way" (BTW) vulnerability. This allowed the retrieval of administrative credentials belonging to the "qala-kabusha" user. These credentials were then used to log into all of the MikroTik RouterOS routers, which gave access to the routing functionality of the international office. However, nothing was pursued further with this as to not disrupt valid operations. A malicious actor however clearly would have eventually compromised the networks of said office.
>
> During the same internal test, a GAC2500 conference room phone was also found to use default credentials, which allowed access to it and to any calls routed through it. The security camera system was also discovered when looking at the open ports. This security camera system similarly still allowed the default credentials, which led to a compromise and viewing of the video.

This international office scenario illustrates several ways by which systems could be compromised once the bad actor is inside the network. I emphasize that in many instances, the only thing separating the external from the internal is time, and time is always on the bad actor's side.

Internal testing is so important that I have elected to show another scenario illustrating why it should be part of a comprehensive penetration test.

Report Narrative

> Webcheck Security tested the discovered open ports and saw that quite a few services were replicated across different servers. A sampling of those services was tested for access, but all failed. Other ports and protocols

were discovered and common attacks such as default credentials were tested on those ports and listening services. Several printers were discovered that did not have any password protecting their administrative interfaces. It is recommended that these have passwords implemented as there has been a rise of attacks against printer/scan/fax machines lately to use them as exfiltration or secondary attack points.

Webcheck Security looked through the rest of the compromised system and discovered two systems that were missing the patch for (OS and App names). These systems were (target names), both systems that appear to be used for financial transactions/trades. This vulnerability was used to completely compromise these systems and install a local administrator account. This account could be used to install malware on these machines that records/changes/deletes transactions that are run through them.

This particular scenario shows that once inside the network, hackers would have inevitably found inroads through an unpatched system, as well as administrative portals for printers that were using default credentials.

Although asset enumeration is an important part of a cybersecurity strategy, it is easy to see how just one machine or device missed on an update or log table can lead to disastrous breach capability, hence strengthening the need for assurance provided by internal testing.

Web Application Testing

Another way to gain access to data, credentials, and systems is through vulnerable web applications. More will be said about web app penetration testing later on, as well as common vulnerabilities, but sometimes, less obvious methods can lead to compromise.

In the following redacted report excerpts, these live web applications we tested provided information exposure that unintentionally led attackers to means of compromise.

SCENARIO 1 REPORT NARRATIVE

Risk Factor: <u>Medium</u>
Description: An information exposure is the intentional or unintentional disclosure of information to an actor that is not explicitly authorized to have access to that information. The information provides data about the application or its environment that could be useful in an attack but is normally not available to the attacker.

Remediation: Only disclose <u>necessary information</u> in responses to applications users.

Additional Detail

Email enumeration possible (See screenshot below)

Did not find your EmailAddress to reset password.

Login Back

*Using a message like the following is suggested: To reset your password (or, if you haven't yet, activated your account), check your inbox and look for our email.

Email

Test@Test.com

Email is already is use

First Name

Tester1'

Last Name

Test

*Consider using error messages that do not disclose database information. SSN / FEIN enumeration possible

SSN / FEIN

555-55-5555

SSN / FEIN is already in use

*Consider using error messages that do not disclose database information.

So in this scenario, if the application reveals that the "email is already in use," the hacker knows that all she has to do is crack the password. That leads to a broadening of the attack surface, since now multiple emails can be attempted and either validated or invalidated, leading to a very large amount of potential credentials to compromise.

Web applications can be so fraught with vulnerabilities that I felt it helpful to include this example of how multiple attack vectors in one application might lead to total system compromise.

SCENARIO 2 REPORT NARRATIVE

Summary of Results

Multiple issues and some sensitive data was discovered as part of the authenticated penetration test though that should be addressed since given enough time would lead to compromise. They are:

1. Internal Git index files are accessible to the outside world, they give a full list of all software installed via Git and give significant sensitive information to an external attacker.
   a. Severity – **HIGH**

2. Two repositories on GitHub are publicly accessible. Although no API keys or passwords were discovered in them, they should be made private as they give source code to an attacker. One of them looked depreciated, but still could provide historical source code.
   a. Severity – **HIGH**

3. Multiple HTTP sites allow username/password submission in cleartext. This could be easily intercepted on a shared public network and these sites should automatically redirect to HTTPS before allowing login.
   a. Severity – **HIGH**

4. The Apache server is version 2.4.6. Although there are no serious vulnerabilities for 2.4.6 yet, it should be upgraded to the most current version when possible (2.4.12).
   a. Severity – **MEDIUM**

5. SSL cookies are not set with "secure" flag. This can lead to session ID compromise should a user go from an HTTPS session to an HTTP session on a shared public network.
   a. Severity – **MEDIUM**

Informational:
Eight email addresses and 12 usernames were discovered as part of the assessment. This is just informational to have XYZ Company be aware and to make sure they have robust passwords. (All usernames are then listed in the report.)

This scenario outlines the multiple risks that can be lurking in web application code, leading to critical data or total system compromise. It is interesting to note how much information about an application was found from a public source, namely the GitHub repository, which could prove to be very damaging to a corporation. Reconnaissance, therefore, is an important part of web application and penetration testing in general. Several pages will be dedicated to the concept of the reconnaissance process as part of good penetration testing outcomes.

Scenario 3 Report Narrative

External Web Application SQL Injection Vulnerability – A SQL injection vulnerability was discovered on a page behind the login portal on the external website. Exploiting it successfully obtained the system username running the web application. No database tables are linked to the page though, so no further compromise was able to be obtained.

Vulnerable Unitrends 9.x Installation Allows for Remote Code Execution on TCP port 1743 – The Unitrends installation located at 10.x.x.x is running a vulnerable version of the Unitrends BPServer software on TCP port 1743 that allows for remote code execution. This allowed for full compromise of the server with root access to the command line. Because it is the backup server, several sensitive passwords were found on the system. These passwords mainly applied to the backup server though, which was already fully compromised.

The small excerpt from this last scenario exposes a vulnerability that we continue to find in so many web applications, known as SQL injection. I will discuss this in more detail as we discuss the Open Web Application Security Project (OWASP) and the OWASP Top Ten.

SSID Testing

Service set identifier (SSID) or Wi-Fi testing is another best practice to ensure systems are secure internally. Stated another way, businesses typically have one or more wireless routers, which also provide obvious potential points of entry for bad actors.

Here is a scenario typical of one we recently found:

The tester performed an assessment of the wireless networks available. SSID enumeration and account security was analyzed. Various attacks were performed, and the encrypted handshakes were retrieved. The password was attempted to be decrypted with several password brute force attacks, but they were all unsuccessful.

A couple wireless SSIDs were discovered that have vulnerabilities, including one with WEP encryption and one using WPS pin passwords. Both of these are easily cracked.

In this case, the passwords were good, but one router had weak encryption and bad passwords enabled, making it easily "hackable."

All of these are typical of scenarios that will be encountered by qualified penetration testers. They underscore the importance of multifaceted approach testing.

Types of Penetration Tests

There are many types of penetration testing. Some of them have been shown in context with the live examples shown previously. I thought it would be helpful to additionally list them here followed by definitions.

Here they are listed in order of what I would consider a prioritized approach:

- External penetration testing
- Web application testing
- Internal penetration testing
- SSID or wireless testing
- Social engineering, including phishing and call campaigns
- Mobile application testing

All of this should be done in all organizations at least annually as applicable. An organization may not have a web or mobile application or login portal which that organization has designed or commissioned, in which case such web app and mobile testing would not apply. Similarly, if no wireless routers exist in the organization, SSID testing is not applicable. Phishing is always applicable, as it has become the number-one source of compromise in organizations.

Here is a brief definition of each element of testing. Each element is tested with the CIA Security Triad objectives in mind, which consists of the following three areas: confidentiality – prevention of unintended disclosure; integrity – assurance that data has not been subject to unauthorized modification; and availability – a resource that is accessible and usable when required:

External Testing – Testing external assets or public-facing IP addresses that are visible to the Internet, such as firewalls, routers, and other accessible servers or devices. The objective is to gain access to internal systems, data, and assets.

Web Application Testing – Thorough authenticated and unauthenticated testing of web applications, portals, or code that has access to sensitive data, or when compromised, may lead to root access to the server and systems.

Internal Penetration Testing – Behind-the-firewall testing of all internal IP addresses or assets with the objective of finding vulnerabilities that will lead to system compromise, access to sensitive data, and disclosure. Such tests must be done with system authentication and access to at least one segment of a network.

SSID or Wireless Testing – Testing of all wireless access points or routers for vulnerabilities and ability to compromise and gain system or data access, particularly where bad passwords or old protocols may be concerned.

Social Engineering, Including Phishing and Call Campaigns – Simulating fraud through email or call campaigns, with the intent to see if users will be fooled into yielding valuable credentials, which could be used in system compromise. Also indicative of whether users are apt to click on "bad" links, which may allow malware or ransomware to be downloaded into the system.

Mobile Application Testing – Testing iOS- or Android-installed applications to find vulnerabilities, loopholes, or other methods of compromise.

Comprehensive penetration testing will often include all of this in larger organizations, at a price tag starting at $20,000 for one web app and just a handful of external and internal IPs and SSIDs. Please note: The small investment in a penetration test and other cybersecurity controls is a small price to pay when compared to the average cost of a data breach, which currently sits at $3.9 million.[3] The investment in a comprehensive pen test, even in a larger scope with a $50,000 price tag, pales in comparison to the potential losses posed by data breach.

Definitions of Low, Medium, High, and Critical Findings in Penetration Testing

You will notice that each of the report excerpts contained designations of medium, high, or critical in the report. These are standard across the penetration test industry among most pen test vendors, but here is how we categorize them at Webcheck Security:

Critical – Test findings that will most likely lead to effective total compromise and having critical impact on the organization. This might involve administrative or root system–level access on a network, server, or servers, or provide access to sensitive information and subsequent data exfiltration. In compliance situations, it could also signify a severe lack of compliance with regulatory bodies, which could lead to fines, penalties, or loss of contractual status and resulting business.

High – Test findings that will indicate a high impact on the enterprise if compromised. Indicates potential for compromise of information systems on a network or servers containing information or documents. In compliance situations, it could also signify a high lack of compliance with regulatory bodies, which could lead to fines, penalties, or loss of contractual status and resulting business.

Medium – Test findings that can immediately lead to compromise of nonpublic data or has the potential to lead to the compromise of data through further exploitation. May document a lack of compliance with industry best practices or standards that could lead to possible logical or physical exploitation, penalties, fines, or other monetary or legal actions as regulatory requirements become stricter, or an operational deficiency that would leverage the company's ability to ensure the confidentiality, integrity, and/or availability of information.

Low – Findings in this category suggest that information could be used in future attempts to compromise any nonpublic data, any finding that does not pose an immediate threat, or documents the minimum required compliance with the regulation/requirement but does not meet industry best practices or standards, and there is potential for improvement.

Informational Only – Items for future review which, due to the contract, may not have been tested or could be used against the company later. For example, denial of service (DoS) and distributed denial of service (DDoS) attacks would fall into this rating category.

Compliances and Frameworks: Pen Testing Required

Penetration testing is more than just a best practice and part of a multifaceted infosec policy. It is required in most compliance and security frameworks. For example, for organizations that fall in the scope of Requirement 11 of payment card industry (PCI), which states "Regularly test security systems and processes," penetration testing is mandatory (see requirement 11.3). The standard then provides very prescriptive guidance. For example, the company or tester chosen to perform the test for PCI compliance must be outside of the company or from a department not managed by compliance, IT, or entities affiliated with the company's cardholder data systems. The entity also has to have industry-recognized certifications such as the CEH, CPT, OSCP, SANS, or other reputable ones.

What follows is a list of common standards and frameworks that require or strongly suggest annual penetration testing. Those with an asterisk are standards for which penetration testing is not optional for full-scope scenarios:

- PCI*
- HIPAA
- ISO 27001*
- SOC 1/SOC 2
- FedRAMP*
- NIST*
- CIS*
- COBIT*
- HITRUST*

Although some certifications such as PCI, FedRAMP, ISO 27001, and HITRUST require penetration testing versus others where quarterly vulnerability scanning is acceptable, if an organization wants to understand how vulnerable it is, then they should hire a penetration tester to find all of the backdoors! I often say a penetration test is the only true way to tell how secure a business really is in a point in time and allows not only vulnerabilities to be revealed but process gaps as well.

For example, let's say a test reveals that you are running a vulnerable operating system (OS) or software. Upon further review you might realize that your IT inventory process as well as patch management may not be up to par, spurring you to implement effective changes.

One word on NIST, mentioned earlier. There is a groundswell movement in the U.S. government to protect itself from attacking nation-states, particularly China, Iran, and Russia. In 2020 a new element is being introduced to the NIST framework in that all defense and government contractors who may have access to nonsensitive, nonclassified data will still have to be Cybersecurity Maturity Model Certification (CMMC) certified. CMMC will be primarily based (for most businesses) on the NIST SP 800-171 or Defense Federal Acquisition Regulation Supplement (DFARS). My point here is that such certification and business continuance will require penetration testing.

OWASP and OWASP Top Ten

The OWASP establishes a baseline of testing, which many companies demand in their penetration testing engagements. OWASP is a nonprofit foundation that works to improve the security of software. Through community-led open-source software projects, hundreds of local chapters worldwide, tens of thousands of members, and leading educational and training conferences, the OWASP Foundation is the source for developers and technologists to secure the Web (https://owasp.org/). OWASP provides tools and resources, community and networking, education, and training.

Recently I spoke to a gentleman responsible for all things IT in his organization. During the conversation, he referred to a critical web application the organization deploys (and which handles sensitive data) but for which they had not hired a third party to conduct a proper penetration test. This is like playing Russian roulette with your web application. When the "bullet" does go off, there will be hurt, and believe me, the bullet will eventually fire.

To illustrate the possibilities of "bullets in the chamber" let's look at the OWASP Top Ten. These are common web application vulnerabilities published each year by the organization. Though the order and priority of these may change over the years, most of these we still find today in all of our web application tests!

OWASP Top Ten with Commentary

1. **Injection** – Injection flaws, such as SQL, NoSQL, OS, and LDAP injection, occur when untrusted data is sent to an interpreter as part of a command or query. The attacker's hostile data can trick the interpreter into executing unintended commands or accessing data without proper authorization.

2. **Broken Authentication** – Application functions related to authentication and session management are often implemented incorrectly, allowing attackers to compromise passwords, keys, or session tokens or to exploit other implementation flaws to assume other users' identities temporarily or permanently.

3. **Sensitive Data Exposure** – Many web applications and application programming interfaces (APIs) do not properly protect sensitive data, such as financial, healthcare, and personally identifiable information (PII). Attackers may steal or modify such weakly protected data to conduct credit card fraud, identity theft, or other crimes. Sensitive data may be compromised without extra protection, such as encryption at rest or in transit, and requires special precautions when exchanged with the browser.

4. **XML External Entities (XXE)** – Many older or poorly configured External Markup Language (XML) processors evaluate external entity references within XML documents. External entities can be used to disclose internal files using the file uniform resource identifier (URI) handler, internal file shares, internal port scanning, remote code execution, and DoS attacks.

5. **Broken Access Control** – Restrictions on what authenticated users are allowed to do are often not properly enforced. Attackers can exploit these flaws to access unauthorized functionality and/or data, such as access other users' accounts, view sensitive files, modify other users' data, change access rights, etc.

6. **Security Misconfiguration** – Security misconfiguration is the most commonly seen issue. This is often a result of insecure default configurations, incomplete or ad hoc configurations, open cloud storage, misconfigured Hypertext Transfer Protocol (HTTP) headers, and verbose error messages containing sensitive information. Not only must all operating systems, frameworks, libraries, and applications be securely configured, but they must be patched and upgraded in a timely fashion.

7. **Cross-Site Scripting (XSS)** – XSS flaws occur whenever an application includes untrusted data in a new web page without proper validation or escaping, or updates an existing web page with user-supplied data using a browser API that can create HTML or JavaScript. XSS allows attackers to execute scripts in the victim's browser that can hijack user sessions, deface websites, or redirect the user to malicious sites.

8. **Insecure Deserialization** – Insecure deserialization often leads to remote code execution. Even if deserialization flaws do not result in remote code execution, they can be used to perform attacks, including replay attacks, injection attacks, and privilege escalation attacks.

9. **Using Components with Known Vulnerabilities** – Components such as libraries, frameworks, and other software modules run with the same privileges as the application. If a vulnerable component is exploited, such an attack can facilitate serious data loss or server takeover. Applications and APIs using

components with known vulnerabilities may undermine application defenses and enable various attacks and impacts.

10. **Insufficient Logging and Monitoring** – Insufficient logging and monitoring, coupled with missing or ineffective integration with incident response (such as services provided by Secuvant Security), allows attackers to further attack systems; maintain persistence; pivot to more systems; and tamper, extract, or destroy data. Most breach studies show time to detect a breach is over 200 days, typically detected by external parties rather than internal processes or monitoring.

Now to my point. These top ten common web application vulnerabilities are only the tip of the iceberg. Penetration testing is an art, and only by hiring a skilled and experienced tester, who will test without organizational bias, can you identify issues such as these, have them documented, and enjoy sound discussion on how to remediate the problems.

Tools of the Trade

Armed with knowledge of types of testing along with OWASP and other methodologies, before we suggest one penetration testing methodology, I felt it helpful to enumerate some of the common tools of the trade. Every tester has a preferred toolset, and here are some common ones.

Even an external-only test will apply half a dozen tools to properly poke and prod an environment for a quality result. This is another tremendous difference between a penetration test and mere vulnerability scanning. The following list is broken out by test phase, which will be described in more detail further on in this chapter.[4]

Reconnaissance Phase	*Research and company study critical to a great pen test*
ARIN	The American Registry for Internet Numbers is the regional Internet registry for Canada, the United States, and many Caribbean and North Atlantic islands. ARIN manages the distribution of Internet number resources, including IPv4 and IPv6 address space and AS numbers.
DNSRecon	DNSRecon provides the ability to perform the following: • Check all NS records for zone transfers • Enumerate general DNS records for a given domain (MX, SOA, NS, A, AAAA, SPF and TXT) • Perform common SRV record enumeration and top-level domain (TLD) expansion

	• Check for wildcard resolution • Brute-force subdomain and host A and AAAA records, given a domain and a wordlist • Perform a PTR record lookup for a given IP range or CIDR • Check DNS server cached records for A, AAAA, and CNAME records, provided a list of host records in a text file to check • Enumerate common mDNS records in the local network enumerate hosts and subdomains using Google
goofile	Allows one to search for a specific file type on a domain, like Excel documents or PowerPoint presentations
goog-mail	Scrapes emails from Google's cached pages
goohost	Extracts hosts/subdomains, IP addresses, and emails from Google for a specific domain
theHarvester	Gathers emails, subdomains, hosts, employee names, open ports, and banners from different public sources
URLCrazy	Looks for domain typos and similar domains
Whois	Public IP verification and possible IT contact
recon-ng	Full framework with multiple modules to find and organize discovered information
Spiderfoot	Comprehensive public record linking OSINT tool
Search engines	Looking for sensitive information
Social Media	LinkedIn, Twitter, Facebook, and job search sites for open positions and tools used
Gitrob	Searches GitHub for sensitive code information
Scanning Phase	*Applying the right tools for various results in the process*
Nmap	Discovers and enumerates open ports
Nikto	Tests web application configurations for misconfigurations and sensitive content
Burp Suite	World-class web application proxy
Gobuster	Directory brute-forcing tool written in GO

OpenVAS	Vulnerability scanner (similar to Nessus or SAINT)
Exploit DB	Public exploit repository
Search engines	Some exploits are not in ExploitDB
Exploit Phase	*Widening the cracks to find more threats for clients to address*
Metasploit	Framework for facilitating exploit attacks
Python, Perl, Bash, C++	For running manual exploits
Netcat	Network communication testing tool
CrackMap	Excellent tool for finding local admin, running Mimikatz, or elevating privileges
Mimikatz	Password exfiltration tool
Responder	NTLMNRR and NetBIOS poisoning tool
Empire PowerShell	PowerShell agent deployment tool for maintaining and increasing access
Deathstar	Automated Windows privilege escalation, data exfiltration tool
Burp Suite	Executing custom web application exploits and brute-force attacks
Hydra	Command-line brute-force tool
Post-Exploit Phase (gaining privileged access and lateral movement)	
Metasploit	Framework for facilitating exploit attacks
Various Linux and Windows scripts to find exploitable weaknesses	
CrackMap	Excellent tool for finding local admin, running Mimikatz, or elevating privileges
NTLMRelay	Pass-the-hash tool for lateral compromise
Cover Tracks/Cleanup Phase	
No specific tools here, this is different enough each time that only manual effort is used.	

As you can see, a good penetration tester will, on an external test only, run many recon tools such as ARIN and DNSRecon, NMAP, then OpenVas, then several other tools in addition to attempted manual exploits.

Pen Test Methodology

Let us take a look at one workflow my vice president (VP) of engineering uses as a checklist, as well as to train other penetration testers. There may be as many ways to perform a penetration test as there are stars in the heavens, especially given that no pen test is created equal. Each will have a different mix of Wi-Fi, SSIDs, internal IPs and segments, externally available ports and services, web apps and methods of access, and infrastructure considerations.

It should be noted here that networking concepts and network administrator knowledge are critical. How do you treat Web Application Firewalls (WAF), load balancers, DNS and Active Directory and run commands in Linux or PowerShell? These are all critical pieces of knowledge to have. Further, some development knowledge, including Python, PHP, JavaScript, and SQL database queries, can be helpful.

Penetration Test Checklist for External IPs and Web Applications[5]

1. Conduct passive recon activity.
   a. Discover.sh from GitHub here: https://github.com/leebaird/discover
2. Find IP address from URL (to see what other ports are open).
   a. Ping URL and pull IP. Ping several times to make sure it isn't a load-balanced IP. If it is, gather a list of all IPs.
3. Nmap IP of single IP.
   a. Use "nmap -p- -A -oG nmap_external_grep.txt {IP Address} > nmap_external_scan.txt"
      i. This will give you a grep file and a scan file of the results
   b. Check UDP too:
      i. "Nmap -sU -A {IP Address} > nmap_external_UDP_scan.txt"
4. Nmap IP of range of IPs discovered earlier.
   a. Use "nmap -p- -A -oG nmap_external_grep.txt -iL {IP list} > nmap_external_scan.txt"
      i. This will give you a grep file and a scan file of the results
   b. Check UDP too:
      i. "Nmap -sU -A -iL {IP list} > nmap_external_UDP_scan.txt"
5. Take a break from the site during the Nmap scan as to not have it miss things; do the passive recon instead.

6. Run Nikto on both the HTTP version and HTTPS version of the URL:
   a. "Nikto --host {Domain name of site - ex: www.google.com} > nikto_http_{site name}.txt"
   b. "Nikto --host {Domain name of site - ex: www.google.com} --ssl --port 443 > nikto_HTTPS_{site name}.txt"
7. Run an OpenVAS scan on the site (this will not get you much, but we are looking for web application software versions for later attacks).
   a. Add a target of the site IP address then run the scan. Wait until it finishes (this can take a long time)
   b. Check out the scan results; sometimes you get lucky and find a heartbleed vulnerability
8. Load up Burp Suite Professional and route web traffic through it via proxy settings. Make sure to tie the site to a save file, do not use a temp session.
9. Visit the site and manually click through every major page and drop-down. THIS IS IMPORTANT! Burp misses things when it spiders the site unless you give it a lot to work with first.
10. Once this is done, if there is a login page, log in to it and click through any remaining new sections of the site that come up.
    a. When you log in, look through the HTTP history right after and note the variable for username and password
11. Put the username and password variable into the Options section of the Spider tab in Burp Suite Professional.
12. Spider the site. If you have put in the variables correctly into the Options tab, very few forms should pop up to fill out. If forms keep popping up asking for username and password, double-check the variable names.
13. Look at your Nikto and Openvas scan results and note the software versions displayed.
14. Run a content brute-force check on the URL. Limit the subdirectories to five or six, leave the other options the same, and add the proper vulnerable list of pages for the web application version you discovered earlier. The vulnerability lists are located here:
    a. /usr/share/wordlists/dirb/vulns/
    b. Let the brute force run all night; it can take a long time. If you notice that after a couple minutes the brute force slows way down, you are likely being throttled by a WAF. Pause the brute force and adjust the delay in milliseconds. Take it 10× slower (so 200 milliseconds instead of 20). See if things steady back out.
    c. Sometimes the brute-force content scanner gets into directory loops due to bad website design. Limiting the subdirectories can help with this, but you can sometimes have tens to hundreds of thousands of pages discovered. You will have to scan through the directory tree structure and delete the trees that are repeats.

15. Once you finally have the brute force done, do an active scan of the entire website. Usually I leave the default options, but it depends if it is 10,000+ web pages. That will take too long, especially if you have to throttle the scanning speed for a WAF. If this happens, unselect the pages without any input fields; that usually is the majority of the scan. Do the scan and see if you find anything good. If you don't, then do another scan of just the pages without any input fields.

At this point you will have a mountain of information to go through, and it depends on what you find to determine the next steps. Here are a couple of key items and what to do to confirm them:

1. Notable pages found in either Nikto file:
    a. Visit each one of these (unless there are hundreds so it is bad website design). These can give you a great deal of good findings. You might find a login page or version info or git repositories, etc. If so, take note of it and try to find out more information.
    b. Look for and try exploits for every vulnerable version you find.
        i. "Searchsploit – update"
        ii. "Searchsploit {software version}"
    c. Take screenshots of anything notable found.
2. OpenVas scan results:
    a. This will usually be outdated version info of the website. Look for exploits for each vulnerable version of software you find.
3. Nmap scan results:
    a. This usually doesn't give much, but it might give other open ports that either give info for the server or should not be open to the Internet.
    b. Be careful here: if only the website is in scope, you should not test any other port except the website ports (usually 80 and 443).
4. Burp scan results:
    a. SQLi results
        i. Integrate your Burp Suite with SQLMapapi by following the instructions here: https://support.portswigger.net/customer/portal/articles/2791040-using-burp-with-sqlmap
        ii. Look at the individual findings. If the sleep command or other SQL command just has the site timeout, that is likely not a SQLi.
    b. Python/OS/generic injection results
        i. These depend on what has been found. Google how to exploit each one and try findings.
    c. SQLi cheatsheet links:
        i. https://www.netsparker.com/blog/web-security/sql-injection-cheat-sheet/
        ii. https://medium.com/@Kan1shka9/pentesterlab-from-sql-injection-to-shell-walkthrough-7b70cd540bc8

       iii. http://niiconsulting.com/checkmate/2014/01/from-sql-injection-to-0wnage-using-sqlmap/

       iv. Manual SQL injection steps without SQLMap: https://medium.com/@hninja049/step-by-step-sql-injection-ed1bb97b3eae

       v. More manual examples: https://resources.infosecinstitute.com/anatomy-of-an-attack-gaining-reverse-shell-from-sql-injection/

  d. XSS (reflected or stored) results:

       i. Load each one into the Repeater tab in Burp.

       ii. Attempt to reproduce the page (sometimes the session ID has expired). If need be, revisit in the browser and send the new page from the HTTP history to the Repeater tab.

       iii. Attempt to get a working proof of concept of the XSS vulnerability. Once you do, note the results and take a screenshot. Create reproduction steps for the developers.

  e. Local/remote file inclusion:

       i. If you find this, you found a reverse shell entry point. Follow the instructions on how to go from LFI/RFI to reverse shell. Here are some guides that can help:

       ii. https://blog.techorganic.com/2012/06/21/lets-kick-shell-ish-part-1-directory-traversal-made-easy/

       iii. https://blog.techorganic.com/2012/06/26/lets-kick-shell-ish-part-2-remote-file-inclusion-shell/

       iv. https://awakened1712.github.io/oscp/oscp-lfi-rfi/

       v. https://www.adampalmer.me/iodigitalsec/2013/08/15/php-local-and-remote-file-inclusion-lfi-rfi-attacks/

  f. CSRF

       i. Send this one to the Repeater tab and attempt to confirm. If you can, take notes and screenshots.

  g. CORS

       i. You will find a lot of these. It depends if you want to report this one; most of the time the client does not understand it whatsoever and the risk is low.

  h. Access to files outside of individual user's rights

       i. Look at the site tree and see if any of the folders or addresses look like they are a number sequence or other procedurally generated number/letter combinations.

       ii. Load one of the pages into the Intruder tab. Clear all fields and then select a field that you want to brute force. Load up a brute-force list or iterate through numbers, then kick off the attack. Look for HTTP 200 pages or for large changes in content amount.

  i. Login pages

       i. These are fun. First, look at the version of the software of the login page and see if it has a default username/password. Try that username/password. See if it warns of a lockout due to failed login attempts.

ii. If it does not have a default password but it does have a default user-name, load the login page into the Intruder tab from a failed login attempt. Change the password field to the field that will rotate. Load in a password list like "Darkc0de" or "RockYou." Set it to look through each response for something to change, like not to have a "failed login" on the page anymore. You will have to look at the response for the failed login to see what message comes up when the login failed. Once that is in place, kick off the attack and look for when the failure notice goes away. That will be the correct password.

j. WAR file/backdoor file admin access

i. If you can get to an admin page and login where you can upload pages, upload a reverse shell. Make sure you tie it to your IP address, though, as you do not want to upload a page that another attacker could use to hack the site.

1. Use a listening netcat port to see if you get a response at first for testing. Just set up the listening port, upload the reverse shell page, visit the page, and see if your netcat port sees any traffic.

k. WordPress sites

i. If you find a WordPress login page, take note of the URL. Use WPSCAN to check for any vulnerable plugins.

1. "Wpscan – update"
2. "Wpscan – url {site URL of login page}"

ii. Sometimes you have to put in a content directory if the site does not follow standard WordPress directory structure format.

As you can see from this thorough process (most of which is geared to web applications; items 1 to 4 and 7 can apply to external IP testing), there is much work to do for a thorough pen test to be effective, and of course this explains the cost of proper penetration testing, as well as clear differences between merely running scans versus employing pen test techniques.

At a high level, we break down our process into four critical components illustrated in the following graphic:

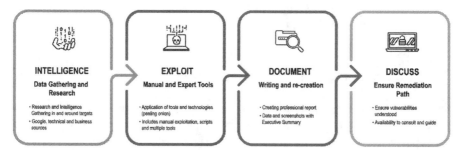

INTELLIGENCE	EXPLOIT	DOCUMENT	DISCUSS
Data Gathering and Research	Manual and Expert Tools	Writing and re-creation	Ensure Remediation Path
• Research and Intelligence Gathering in and around targets • Google, technical and business sources	• Application of tools and technologies (peeling onion) • Includes manual exploitation, scripts and multiple tools	• Creating professional report • Data and screenshots with Executive Summary	• Ensure vulnerabilities understood • Availability to consult and guide

Intelligence. During the Intelligence phase, data is gathered not just about the targets being tested through recon tools, but also research on the company itself is performed. This research may reveal potential user IDs, password possibilities, and in many cases other unprotected IP data that is "hanging out there" and might be exploited.

Exploit. This is, of course, a critical component of penetration testing. As observed in the test script on the previous page, the ability to find and then further exploit the vulnerabilities, or "peeling the next onion layer," is how loopholes and problems are found. My associate Curt always says that good pen testers are problem solvers. They enjoy a challenge and seek for nuggets to exploit and document.

Documentation. This phase may be just as critical as the actual exploitation. After all, it won't help your client if you can't describe (1) what you found, (2) how you got there, and (3) how they fix it! Clear and concise writing with good, easy-to-follow vulnerability descriptions and remediation advice will be critical.

Including screenshots in a professionally formatted report is also a critical component of the documentation phase. I've included a sample in the ensuing page to illustrate the "nice touch" that a sharp report can provide.

You will notice in the table of contents that the report has an Executive Summary, a Conclusion and Risk Rating section, and a clear Recommendations section. Each of these has a critical purpose for a client, but of these, the Executive Summary and Recommendations are the most important.

The client's clients will often ask for proof of a penetration test, and the Executive Summary is what can be sent rather than the comprehensive detail found in the full report. Second, a clear Recommendations page will help the client understand exactly what needs to be done in order to remediate the findings (Figure 3.1).

Discussion. This is the "extra mile" phase. It not only is in place to ensure clients get the consultation they need and deserve to understand test results but are clear on exactly what steps or direction must be taken to resolve key findings.

For many penetration testers, the organization tasks them with cranking out reports or are themselves obsessed with merely this level and miss the opportunity to enhance the customer experience and really add value to the penetration test deliverable and outcome.

It could be said that this phase flows throughout the test, since important findings really should be communicated to clients promptly in order to facilitate prompt action and quickly reduce existing vulnerabilities.

Chapter Takeaways

Now you should have greater insight into penetration testing, tools, methods, and standards that require it. I started the chapter with some scenarios where real exploitable attack vectors were found. Let me finish with one as well.

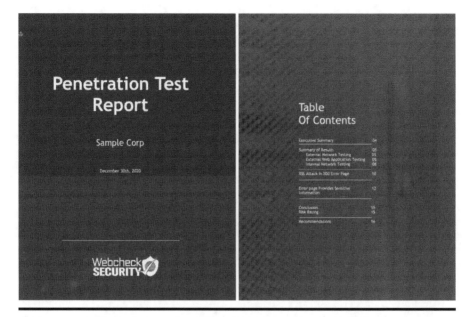

Figure 3.1   Webcheck Security title and contents pages. All Rights Reserved.

In my first real cybersecurity gig years ago, a client, a small but successful Mexican restaurant in the Southwest, was hacked and for at least three months had been bleeding its clients' credit card data. They only came to my company because they a digital forensic investigation was required through their card processor by MasterCard, who had triangulated the data loss and fraud to their restaurant.

The outcome was not good. MasterCard levied a fine of $80,000, assessed through the acquiring bank or processor. In this scenario, if one chooses not to pay, your account is garnished until it is and your processing privileges shut off. We all know how annoying it is to go to pay for food only to be told "We accept cash only." Hence not a good option.

The outcome of this scenario was not good. Not long after the forensic investigation was completed, the restaurant went out of business. Multiply that little $80,000 fine by 10 or even 100. If it's not uncommon for an *average* data breach cost to be $3.9 million in the United States, those numbers could be catastrophic.

Contrast the $80,000 to what may have been less than $5,000 for a one- or two-IP address penetration test – a test that would certainly have uncovered the vulnerabilities, which in this case the hacker used to deposit malware and a rogue FTP server on the POS server (a Remote Desktop Protocol [RDP] desktop was open, by the way).

This final narrative in this chapter serves to summarize the key message here, which is annual or semi-annual penetration testing is a small fee compared to the alternative.

Resources

1 arXiv:1701.04940v1 [cs.CR] 18 Jan 2017; https://arxiv.org/pdf/1701.04940.pdf
2 M-Trends 2019: Celebrating 10 Years of Incident Response Reporting; https://www.fireeye.com/blog/executive-perspective/2019/03/mtrends-2019-celebrating-ten-years-of-incident-response-reporting.html
3 IBM in conjunction with the Ponemon Institute https://databreachcalculator.mybluemix.net/
4 Source: Curt Jeppson, VP Engineering, Webcheck Security and expert cyber practitioner.
5 Ibid, Curt Jeppson.

Chapter 4

Threat Hunting

In this chapter we introduce threat hunting primarily from the perspective of a security operations group, or in other words a full security operations center (SOC; something I call the MI6 room) and how such activities can prevent a cyber disaster. The principles discussed in this chapter are the most effective with the right tools, techniques, and threat hunter qualities.

It should be noted that the tools, resources, and time to build full SOC operations (hence, effective threat hunting) can be costly and is often accomplished by organizations in excess of a billion in revenue. Below that, organizations will outsource these services, and for good reason. If an organization only hires one analyst and licenses one security information and event manager (SIEM) software product (a critical piece of the threat hunter's toolkit), the costs have already skyrocketed to a minimum of $200,000 per year in a smaller organization – and the analyst will only be there during business hours. Outsourcing of the threat hunting component on a subscription basis is therefore an extremely attractive, affordable, and viable option for most organizations!

You will see from the tales and threat intel in this chapter that for organizations where intellectual property, data, brand, compliance, and other risk is high, a threat hunting operation can be essential. In fact, one way to define threat hunting is with this simple definition:

> Threat hunting is reducing bad actor dwell time in assets and systems of an organization from the average of 200 days to less than a week. This is accomplished by trained security analysts using advanced tools and cyber triage* knowledge.
>
> *Triage – The ability to effectively identify, classify, and report on cyber threats.

Without threat hunters armed with the appropriate training and tools, cyber events can wreak havoc on businesses, schools, government, nonprofits – any kind of organization.

A SOC's automated tools will miss things. Malicious actors use new concepts and attack vectors every day, and the rules and algorithms raising alerts sometimes take time to catch up. Threat hunting catches events that are missed by automated alerts, and these can be turned into use cases to modify the SOC rules so an alert is automatically generated for similar occurrences in the future.

Not-So-Tall Tales

First some threat hunting stories based on real events. These are stories I have documented over the years from various sources, though the sources, as well as the names of people and companies involved, are not identified here for obvious reasons. Some embellishment of the narrative has been added to better illustrate the core events:

> Joe was a typical successful executive of a medical and aerospace contractor. He had hired good personnel – requests for proposals (RFP) writers, business development specialists, and, of course, a great manufacturing crew – all contributing to engage and win business in their sector.
>
> Joe and his leadership team often celebrate their wins with an afternoon of 18 holes at the local country club. This year was shaping up to be no different, with several wins under their belts and a multimillion-dollar manufacturing RFP, which had been written to showcase the strengths of his company's products.
>
> His business development and writing team were just putting the finishing touches on the proposal, and Friday afternoon looked beautiful, so he grabbed Fred and Jim, the chief financial officer (CFO) and chief operations officer (COO), respectively, and went off to play 18 holes for the rest of the day. It was a good day.
>
> Unbeknownst to Joe and his team however, Sally, their normally sharp executive assistant, had unwittingly clicked on a fake email link several months earlier, leading to the Emotet Trojan slowly working its way through the system and giving a bad actor access to systems and data, even installing rootkits along the way.
>
> Monday morning Joe, his team, and all employees were dismayed when they tried to access the RFP to send it off to their prospective client. Today was the deadline. This is what popped up on the screen:
> *This disk has been encrypted. Check your email.*

"What on earth is going on?" thought Joe as he opened his email account. Then this email was at the top of his inbox:

Please pay careful attention to this email.

- *I have downloaded approximately 959 SSNs from your HR server.*
- *I have customer names and prospective customers from your ERP system.*
- *I have downloaded machine tooling data from your servers*
- *You will wire me $25,000 in Bitcoin*
- *Further if you do not do this, I will contact your customers and tell them their proprietary designs were breached*
- *I will then sell your medical device designs to China*

Oh, and by the way, your executives' SSN numbers are as follows (he lists their Social Security numbers.)

Joe and his team were flabbergasted. "Is this some kind of hoax? How do we address this?" After careful discussion with his team, they called Adam in IT and asked him to fix things. Adam toiled all day but without success. Alas, the team didn't have proper backups. As 5:00 rolled around and the RFP deadline came and went, no data was able to be restored. They thought that perhaps over time they might restore some of the data from personal hard drives....

...two weeks later, another email came in from the hacker:

Dear Mr. CEO and Executive Team: I see from your emails that you have not taken me seriously nor has my ransom been paid. It's a shame you missed out on that $50 million-dollar RFP isn't it? Oh – and tell Sally she can't have Wednesday off as she requested (see – I am in your emails).

Because you didn't take me seriously, I downloaded an additional 40 GB of product designs and data from your design folder. I've downloaded 15 years of employee bank account numbers. Oh, and Joe, you Fred and Jim need to stop golfing and pay attention to my demands. BTW – here are your salaries: (States executives' salaries to prove he has been in payroll.)

Not such a good outcome for this company. This is an example of one *without* a threat hunting team or service. Here are several condensed narratives showing what can happen to prevent disasters such as this one:

Harry was a great director of IT. Widgets, Inc.'s operations ran smoothly, and several years ago, having the foresight to recognize the risks in their manufacturing environment, he reached out to a third party and subscribed to their threat detection and threat hunting service. Such proved to be a "bacon-saver!"

Harry was closing a deal on a house, so when the Docusign email showed up, thinking it was related to such, he clicked on it, opened the link to what looked like the Docusign login, and entered his credentials. "This one must be defective," he thought, since up came a blank screen and nothing happened. "I guess I'll talk to my realtor later."

Harry then realized he was late to a meeting so left his computer (which was downloading malware) and went to the meeting. By the time the meeting was over, it was 5:00 and a Friday afternoon, so he shut down his computer and left. Unbeknownst to him, his compromised system then invited malware to download from a server it had branched to.

Thank heavens for the third-party SOC subscription Harry had subscribed to! The SOC operation during this time reported this narrative:

- At about 7 PM, after-hours when everyone had left office, we received an automated alert from our chat system about a high-score network threat event at Widgets, Inc.
- I began triage, started following our response procedure, and sent a standard alarm to the client.
- I took a closer look at what looked like a malware alert, so I looked at the malware and performed a manual analysis, confirmed the family and functionality of malware, and verified the installation was successful and the infected device was beaconing out.
- I escalated the severity and notified the client because of grave risk of data theft. Taken in context with the risk exposure of Widgets, Inc. being aerospace, I made a call to after-hours to escalate via phone.
- Our client immediately engaged, removed the machine from the network, and consequently the threat of lateral movement or data exfiltration.
- Malware was detected, analyzed, classified, and removed within 1.5 hours afterhours.

What would Harry have done as the IT director had the company been severely damaged in this scenario due to ransomware, data exfiltration, brand tarnishing, or legal and other implications? Clearly, the systems in place along with this threat hunter reduced dwell time and, even better, completely circumvented a potential tragedy within 1.5 hours.

Similarly, these ensuing bullet-point narratives from two different SOCs show an analyst's perspective (the threat hunter) and demonstrate not only insight into the threat hunting process but the clear benefits of threat hunting in an organization:

- **Company 1 – A Phishing Spree**
  - Correlated multiple independent phishing attempts into a more significant campaign that affected the company broadly.
  - We escalated the severity of multiple, individual successful phishing attacks to CRITICAL from HIGH due to our observations and correlation.
  - We initiated the client calling tree and validated with the client that they received our tickets and were engaged in a response procedure.
- **Company 2 – OS X Torrenting**
  - We received an alert on Tor being used in a client network. We investigated the activity a bit deeper. In reviewing the network history of the device that made the suspicious connections, we observed connections to an internet relay chat (IRC) network. Specifically, they had connected to a channel named "Olarila."
  - Using this information, we generated an alarm to the client that a user was actively connecting to Tor under suspicious conditions. We discovered that Olarila is actually an online project that allows people to pirate copies of OS X for virtualization.
  - We confirmed illegal activity and notified the client that IT staff were obtaining illegal resources via Tor. We confirmed that OS X was being pirated over Tor and that a user was confirmed to be interacting with a community created for illegal acts. The IT manager went through a more official route to remove the OS images and confirmed the issue was an instance of shadow IT.
  - We confirmed the incident timeline. Root cause: IT staff was tasked with vetting out an Apple technology and needed a copy of OS X. A user wasn't provided with adequate resources, found illegal copies online himself, and under his own volition downloaded Tor to proceed with the illegal download. The client confirmed this was shadow IT engaging in risky behavior.
- **Company 3 – CC Exfil False Positive (with all the events, someone needs to filter!)**
  - We received an alert that the network threat sensor was observing credit cards in the network stream.
  - We found out it was absolutely a false positive and confirmed that both the originator and the destination were hosts expected to be communicating with each other.
  - We confirmed that the communications were not malicious and that there was a business use case for those communications. We updated the whitelist to silence future alerts of this type.
- **Company 4 – Bad SurveyMonkey**
  - XYZ Clinics has a major issue with phishing/scam emails. They have negative IT operations capacity and rely on our expertise to verify if a suspicious email is malicious or not. There have been some interesting

confirmations both for false-positive and confirmed malicious, but we provide manual analysis to verify.

– The nature of the phishing messages was an obfuscated link to SurveyMonkey asking for financial documents to be uploaded through a random tool to some random organization.

– Spoofed email addresses were being used to communicate financial requests to XYZ employees. They were intended to look like users from within the organization or affiliated with it, but were sending the email addresses using external addresses. The content of the emails indicated that they had internal information about the company's processes and tactics for sending wire transfers. There were deliberate attempts to commit wire fraud against XYZ employees.

Reviewing logs from their email system, we were able to verify that a user had logins coming from Nigeria that matched up with what looked like an email compromise. We conclusively determined the user's credentials were compromised and had XYZ engage in a broad remediation to reset passwords and clear all established sessions to ensure the attacker lost persistence. Remediation did stop all malicious login activity, and the malicious wire fraud emails ceased.

▪ **Company 5 – Spam Infections**

– Monitoring spawned an incident response.

– ABC company got several infections on <date>. At least six machines were nearly simultaneously infected and showing command/control behavior. Client engaged us due to an excessive volume of failed logins, and we received an intrusion detection system (IDS) alert while they were on the phone.

– We began analysis and determined the initial scope was critical. We had previously provided action items for the client to follow that they had neglected.

– The following Monday they received another series of IDS notifications about spam software beaconing out from a few different machines. Got a list of four hosts that were observed sending beacons. Created a triage priority and advised on containment and eradication procedures for the incident. Client performed them and reported back. We advised to isolate and remediate a SQL server first and then to remediate the other hosts beaconing out. Their primary Domain Controller (DC) then made a suspicious Domain Name Server (DNS) request that seemed to involve Mail Exchange (MX) records, and given the spam nature of these attacks, was very concerning.

– Counsel was engaged, and they determined incident response was necessary. We worked with the incident response firm to hand off the incident, providing them with relevant data and information and ensuring a prompt and thorough initiation of the engagement.

As one can see from these narratives, threat hunters wear capes (or should). They are truly superheroes and can save the day in many instances. The events described here saved the organizations millions of dollars to include legal liability, business disruption, and brand tarnishment.

Nation-State Bad Actors: China and Iran

The threats described on the previous pages are prevalent in the United States, but compounding the threat landscape are nation-states who want nothing more than to steal corporate secrets from American business (and its allies) – and don't think you're safe if your business is small.

Even as the manuscript for this book was being prepared, on January 3, 2020, a U.S. airstrike killed Iranian Major General Soleimani. Iran then responded by bombing two U.S. bases in Iraq. Even though the months following these events were considered a time of de-escalation, the U.S. intelligence community predicted cyber retaliation (see https://unit42.paloaltonetworks.com/threat-brief-iranian-linked-cyber-operations/).

Did this cyber retaliation occur? You be the judge. Here is just one account of real events that were observed in the weeks following the attack, in just one SOC:

- Client 1 – Successful GET request originating from Iran
- Client 2 – Failed password for username root from Iran
- Client 3 – [Informational] SMB attempted inbound traffic blocked (185 Kb from Iran)
- Client 4 – Spam email sent from Iran to client
- Client 5 – Web traffic from Iran
- Client 6 – Suspicious domain access
- Client 7 – Unusual connections to Iran

Clearly the nation-state of Iran was poking at more than just the few clients of this particular SOC. Nation-states often have complete call center–type environments full of young eager hackers, banging away at thousands of U.S. IP addresses looking for loopholes and vulnerabilities to exploit.

Which leads us to China. Also while preparing the manuscript for this book, I was invited to attend an FBI briefing on the China threat. It was fascinating and quite an eye-opener. To preface the "China cyber threat," it should be noted that the annual cost to the U.S. economy of counterfeit goods, pirated software, and theft of trade secrets is $225 to $600 *billion*![1]

Also according to this report, the *Made in China 2025 Plan* "lists 10 domestic Chinese industries in which China seeks to significantly reduce its reliance on foreign-produced technology and develop 70% of the components for these projects in China":

- Information technology
- Computer numerical control machine tools and robotics

- Aerospace equipment
- Electric power equipment
- Marine engineering equipment and high-tech ships
- Agricultural equipment
- Advanced rail transportation equipment
- New materials
- Energy-efficient and new-energy automobiles
- Biomedicine and high-performance medical instruments

In the presentation I attended, one might sum up China's strategy using the 3 Rs:

- Rip off
- Replicate
- Replace

In other words, the main goal here is to steal IP and technology, as well as critical information leading to the goals to replicate it and then replace all American tech with the stolen and replicated tech.

Targeted hacking, of course, represents one of the main forms of information theft, and hence threat hunting is a critical defense activity.

Threat Hunting Methods

An esteemed threat hunter associate of mine describes his threat hunting this way:

I typically try to focus on three different types of threat hunting: intelligence based, TTP (tools, techniques, and procedures) based, and trend based. Each method has its own strengths:

Intelligence Based – This method is based on intelligence feeds and news articles (this can be as simple as hearing of a malicious IP in the news and seeing if we can find any hosts reaching out to it [the client environment] in the SIEM). This is the best method to hunt for new attacks and malware. My personal favorite sources for this are the Cyberwire Podcast, the SANS ISC podcast, and the Cisco Talos blog (https://blog.talosintelligence.com/)

TTP (Tools, Techniques, and Procedures) Based – This typically includes using the MITRE ATT&CK Framework (https://mitre-attack.github.io/caret/#/) to follow different attack methods and try to develop ways we can detect them using our toolset. This method can be used to find more advanced attacks that are harder to detect. There are other frameworks, such as Lockheed Martin's Cyber Killchain, but the MITRE ATT&CK framework is generally accepted as the industry de facto standard.

Trend Based – This method involves looking at trends from weekly reports, monthly reports, etc., and looking for anomalies. A spike in failed logins or a change in weekly admin activity can give us a thread to pull on and dig into. This method offers threat hunting that is more personalized to the customer's environment and can detect things that may look like normal traffic to the other methods mentioned earlier.

MITRE ATT&CK

The MITRE ATT&CK framework is a globally accessible knowledge base of bad actor tactics and techniques based on real-world observations. The ATT&CK knowledge base is used as a foundation for the development of specific threat models and methodologies in the private sector, in government, and in the cybersecurity product and service community.[2]

The result is that SIEM tools, manual threat-hunting tactics, and reporting can become more thorough, uniform, and even automated using a universally accepted framework. It will also make the reporting process easier.

Attack techniques and incidents can generally be categorized into one of ten categories: initial access, execution, persistence, privilege escalation, defense evasion, credential access, discovery, lateral movement, collection, exfiltration, command and control, and tools (general and specific). To view a comprehensive table, please see https://attack.mitre.org/.

Technology Tools

It will also be helpful to define some terms and list some of the core tools utilized in the threat hunting process. In doing so please read on with a forgiving heart, as the literally thousands of cyber tools, vendors, techniques, and products would fill volumes, and in identifying some I am leaving many out. This is also not an advertisement or endorsement of any particular technology.

The SIEM

I recently participated in an evaluation of SIEM products. Some of the products reviewed were (listed in no particular order):

- Fortinet FortiSIEM
- Netsurion EventTracker
- Rapid7's SIEM
- AT&T AlienVault
- TrendMicro Cysiv
- SolarWinds Threat Monitor
- AlertLogic SIEM

And that is the tip of the iceberg. One can literally quadruple that product list. Each has its merits and strengths, but for the purposes of this chapter, suffice it to say that a SIEM is at the core of the threat hunt, as logs are stored, categorized, and can be cross-correlated to lead to more findings. Hence, at least in the context of threat hunting in a SOC environment, the SIEM is at the core.

So let's start with SIEM. The SIEM ingests logs from multiple sources: firewalls, virtual machines, cloud app logs such as Office 365, wireless access points, routers, servers of all kinds (web, DNS, authentication, application, Windows, Linux, FTP, mail, etc.), and many other types of devices.

SIEM is at the heart of managed detection and response (MDR). Another concept of MDR is "eyes-on-glass," meaning someone's got your back. Someone is "watching the shop" or in other words looking at critical alerts. This is critical, since most organizations have operational IT, and the nature of operational IT is that of keeping the business running. Hence, since they don't have the bandwidth to monitor the security of the organization 24/7/365, a layer of qualified personnel doing MDR is critical. MDR is threat hunting and responding.

Threat hunters don't go it alone, however. Literally millions of events can occur in one day on just one network alone, and all of those logs are sent to and indexed by the SIEM. Because the aforementioned SIEM products (and all others not mentioned) have complex anomaly detection algorithms and heuristics, alerts get generated automatically, and threat hunters then dive into these, verifying whether events are a false positive or actual event of concern.

It should be noted here that many of the compliances listed in Chapter 3 are fulfilled by the log collection and monitoring provided by SIEM systems. I would caution, however, that log collection without advanced SIEM analytics and threat hunters is merely checkbox-compliance exercise. It is ineffective for true security purposes. As you learned from the scenarios at the beginning of the chapter, and as you will see from the thorough threat hunting process documented further on, log monitoring without SIEM and trained analysts is not security.

EDR

Firewall and server logs don't tell all, however. As demonstrated by the stories at the beginning of this chapter, unwitting users may click on bad stuff. Great technologies are out there to often detect and block bad behavior on user machines. This started decades ago as antivirus protection, but has evolved into a new category of protection known as endpoint protection and endpoint detection and response (EDR).

EDR also involves sending alerts to analysts to review and incorporates not just antivirus and antimalware but also advanced heuristics and often user and entity behavior analytics (UEBA) algorithms. Software that employs UEBA essentially analyzes user activity data from logs, network traffic, and endpoints and correlates such data with threat intelligence to identify activities or behaviors that most likely indicate a malicious threat in the environment.

EDR + SIEM

EDR products are also proliferous and are incorporating advanced artificial intelligence. Sophos, Crowdstrike, Cylance, Carbon Black, Sentinal One, TrendMicro, and others are all examples of advanced EDR technologies. The beauty of them is that most of the SIEM products ingest the logs or alerts of the EDR products, leading to two amazing technologies functioning to increase what I call the incident visibility window.

IDS

Now imagine the aforementioned visibility window widened by yet another technology: an IDS. Many products in this category also exist – and you guessed it – can forward logs and alerts to the SIEM.

Other terms for IDS are bitstream analytics, deep or full packet inspection, partial packet or metadata inspection, and sometimes netflow. Regardless of the technology, the concept is that packets are inspected as they come in from the firewall, both ingress and egress, so that bad stuff or data exfiltration can be detected and alerts sent to the threat hunter.

Common examples of host-based IDS systems are Snort, Suricata, Verizon's ProtectWise, Bro, SecurityOnion, and most of the SIEM systems already mentioned. Fortinet, Palo Alto, Checkpoint, Sonic, Cisco, and most firewalls also have IDS built into them at either basic or very advanced levels.

When 1 + 1 + 1 = 1: The Visibility Window

Where threat hunters can excel will be in an advanced SOC environment where SIEM, EDR, and IDS are functioning as a trifecta and acting as one. Machines beaconing out because they've been taken over as a bot or infected with malware will be detected quickly if there is good bitstream analytics or IDS; then logs can be correlated to determine what other methods of attack might have been used. Phishing attempts can be blocked or detected quickly by EDR and cross-correlated in the SIEM to other potential attacks. Malware coming into the firewall can be quickly detected by the bitstream analytics or, in reverse, packets of database info going out through the firewall can be quickly alerted on.

Such a trifecta (SIEM, EDR, IDS) is almost a necessity for threat hunters in medium- or high-risk environments such as the fintech arena, defense contractors, law firms, healthcare, and manufacturers with intellectual property. With such an enhanced visibility window, threat hunters armed with such tools can do much prevention and detection, averting much damage!

Though some esteemed vendors such as Sophos and others are claiming the industry is moving to the edge and EDR will be more of the future for threat hunters, there still remains a strong argument for the comprehensive, quickly searchable index of logs (think threat incidents) retained by the SIEM, including the implications for digital forensic investigations. Further, the advanced evolution of the SIEM also implies a robust platform for cross-correlative threat hunting.

Threat Hunting Process or Model

The following discovery process demonstrates the steps a good threat hunter might take as he seeks to answer questions about an event. This threat hunting model incorporates SIEM as a basis:

1. What is the event/alert (beaconing, malware, successful login from strange location)?
2. What are the event details?
   a. What is the timestamp?
   b. What is the source IP?
   c. Were elevated privileges gained?
   d. What user information?
   e. What ports and protocols are involved?
3. What is the severity of the event?
   a. Severity level on 1 to 100 scale?
   b. Kill chain stage observation?
      i. Reconnaissance
      ii. Intrusion
      iii. Exploitation
      iv. Privilege escalation
      v. Lateral movement
      vi. Obfuscation/antiforensics
      vii. Denial of service
      viii. Exfiltration
4. Destination IPs
   a. Category: Malware or other?
   b. WhoIS or DNS?
   c. IP reputation?
5. What is the payload?
   a. Review streamheads
   b. Download PCAP information if necessary and available (full packet IDS)
   c. What is the file size and type?
   d. Hash information
6. Network threat sensor observations
   a. What intel rule was matched?

7. Drawing conclusions
    a. No conclusive results? Ticket not raised.
    b. Threat? Ticket raised and triage begins.

The steps in the process all lead to a conclusion of false positive or informational only, or yes, there is a threat and let's raise the alert and begin triage. But the process doesn't end there. Follow-up threat hunting may reveal more useful information.

Surrounding the event that was taken to conclusion, the threat hunter can then begin to do the following:

1. Ask the question, What else is this source IP doing?
    a. Review the source IP of the event in the SIEM.
    b. Correlate username, IP, machine/hostname.
    c. Are there corresponding firewall threats: URL or other?
2. What other indicators of compromise are present?
    a. Look at antivirus or EDR logs, which may correlate.
    b. What additional network threats might be found with that IP or destination?
    c. Is there strange traffic over common ports such as 80, 443, or 53 or an unusual amount of egress traffic over 21, 22, 23, etc.?
    d. Large amounts of DNS traffic from a user's machine?
    e. HTTP traffic with commands in the URL?
    f. Unusual, even misspelled, user agents and strings?
3. Repeat as necessary with other source or destination IPs, common payloads, or other factors.

As you will observe, there could be many other events and more depth to discovered events than was originally found. Threat actors are sneaky and desperate, though not always impatient. Hence, the additional threat hunting activity that might occur, spurred by the initial threat hunting procedure, can yield more three-dimensional data on the state of the enterprise threat posture. Stated another way, the subsequent *secondary* or *expanded* threat process may uncover additional indicators of compromise and lead to more critical findings. Here's a simple example:

Let's say malware is discovered and isolated, and based on IDS and SIEM data, the source IP is identified. Then using telemetry from the first procedures, it is determined that the source IP also made several successful or unsuccessful logins to the user's Office 365 account. That might spawn a search in the SIEM of any successful logins by that IP address to any Office 365 account. The results could be astonishing and result in a quick blocking of said IP, as well as an urgent notification to the users of any successful logins to change their passwords, turn on multifactor authentication (MFA), and ensure the new password is sufficiently long and includes a mix of caps, numbers, characters, etc. Day saved by the threat hunter in the cape!

On Becoming a Threat Hunter

How does one become a threat hunter and/or what skills are necessary to be successful in the field? As mentioned in Chapter 3, a critical skill is the enjoyment of and aptitude for problem solving. The ability to be inquisitive, patient, ask questions, and attempt to draw conclusions will guide the analyst to a successful career.

The Infosec Institute defines five very specific skills that are worth mentioning here, which contribute to the success of a threat hunter:[3]

1. Pattern recognition
2. Data analytics
3. Malware analysis
4. Data forensics
5. Communication

I would say that an aptitude for problem solving and an analytical mind will lay the foundation to enhance or acquire the skills enumerated here, but of them all, communication is the most important. Here, the analogy of the brilliant doctor comes to mind. I don't care how brilliant my doctor is. Does he or she care enough to explain a condition to me in a way that helps me? Does he or she think of ways to solve my problems and provide the best care? This aptly applies to the threat hunter. Does she or he care enough to carefully research, diagnose, and then articulately broadcast the problem, following up to ensure the cyber safety of the organization? Writing and communication skills are critical in this scenario.

I would also recommend to the reader two additional organizations for learning, training, and certification: SANS and ISACA (more info can be found at https://www.sans.org/ and www.isaca.org).

Additionally, (ISC)[2], which is responsible for the respected CISSP certification, is a commendable organization (https://www.isc2.org/). The CISSP itself involves many aspects of cybersecurity, which help to round out the security analyst's cyber view and effectiveness.

The CISSP covers key domains of cybersecurity such as:

Domain 1. Security and risk management
Domain 2. Asset security
Domain 3. Security architecture and engineering
Domain 4. Communication and network security
Domain 5. Identity and access management (IAM)
Domain 6. Security assessment and testing
Domain 7. Security operations
Domain 8. Software development security

Although not all analysts have or need their CISSP, many of the effective analysts I have worked with over the years have possessed this certification. My observation is that it gives practitioners a more holistic view of the cyber landscape.

Threat Hunting Conclusions

Threat hunting is an enterprise-saving activity that detects cyber events and anomalies that have the intent to do harm. Threat hunting is a tremendous defense against standard attacker dwell time. A managed SIEM/SOC solution can viably be outsourced on a subscription basis.

Using advanced threat hunting processes, tools, and techniques, the threat hunter can verify or detect threats in real time, as well as discover other events and anomalies that may have gone undetected by all of the artificial intelligence (AI) and heuristic technology, thus reducing attacker dwell time in systems.

Threat hunters and SOC services are needed – the threats are real, as demonstrated in the scenarios presented. Further, nation-states are involved in espionage and cyberattacks with the intent to acquire data, do harm, and further their initiatives.

The SIEM technology is at the heart of threat hunting and MDR activities and can be enhanced with many other tools and technologies such as EDR, IDS, UEBA, etc.

The SANS, ISACA, and (ISC)² are good sources for threat hunting career growth and multiple certifications.

Resources

1 Federal Bureau of Investigation Handout: *China, the Risk to Corporate America.*
2 See https://attack.mitre.org/
3 *Threat Hunting Careers.* https://resources.infosecinstitute.com/category/enterprise/threat-hunting/threat-hunting-careers/#gref

Chapter 5

Conclusions

As was mentioned at the beginning of Chapter 1, the web applications of today are far more complex and sophisticated than when they were first conceived and developed back during the mid-1990s, during the height of the .com craze. Back then, as long as a web app had a simple e-commerce front, that was all that was needed to get the attention of not only venture capitalists but, most importantly, customers and their repeat business.

Today, there is so much more to a web application than just its front-facing site. There is the back end, which can consist of many complex databases, where some of the most sensitive information and data are stored. This can consist primarily of your customers' financial information, such as credit card numbers, and banking information, and other relevant forms of personally identifiable information (PII).

Of course, just as important, is the server that the web applications reside on. The image of them residing in a physical server has now dissipated; rather, they are stored on virtual machines that are housed in the cloud.

Even the source code that is used to create the web application has become quite complex, and many of the lines of the relevant code that are needed to create it are now outsourced to external third parties for rapid creation and development.

So, as one can see, security across a typical web application encompasses a plethora of areas, ranging from securing the source code, to the virtual machine, to the Internet connectivity that takes place from the device of the end user to the server that houses the web application and vice-versa.

Chapter 1, which dealt with the topic of network security for the web application, covered the following topics:

- A chronological history of the Internet
- The evolution of web applications
- The fundamentals of network security – the OSI model
- Assessing a threat to a web application

- Network security terminology
- The types of network security topologies best suited for web applications
- The types of attacks that can take place against web applications
- How to protect web applications from distributed denial of service (DDoS) attacks
- Defending web applications at a deeper level
- How to properly implement a firewall to safeguard the web application
- The use of intrusion detection systems
- The use of virtual private networks (VPNs) to protect a web application server
- How to assess the current state of security of a web application server
- How to conduct the initial security assessment on the web application
- The techniques that are used by the cyberattacker against the web application and the web application server
- Network security and its relevance for web apps
- Data confidentiality
- Encrypting data in flight
- The Transport Layer Security (TLS) protocol
- Digital certificates
- Setting up network-based sessions
- Finishing the network handshake
- Site validity: Proving your web app is what it says it is
- Testing Your web app's confidentiality and trust
- Spoofing and related concerns

Based on this list, network security is thus a very crucial aspect when it comes to fortifying a secure line of network communications between the virtual machine that houses the web application and the device of the end user that is accessing this particular web application.

But as important as this is, it is equally, if not more, important to further secure the endpoints of this network line of communications, as this is very often overlooked in the design of a web application. As a result, this becomes a prime target for the cyberattacker to pounce upon.

As it has been reviewed, there are many areas, both internally and externally, that a web application needs to be protected from. As Chapter 1 noted, the flow of network communications from the device of the end user and the server that houses the web application (and vice-versa) must be protected. But it is important to keep in mind that a lot of confidential information and data are transmitted across this network medium.

This kind of data is also known as "personable identifiable information" (PII). Typical examples of this include credit card information, banking data, Social Security numbers, driver's license numbers, etc. Take the example of a business that makes use of an e-commerce front, also known as the online store. In these instances, the end user (the customer) will be making purchases from this storefront, most likely using his or her credit card.

While the actual transmission of this data will be sent over a secure network connection (primarily that of the Secure Sockets Layer [SSL]), there are reasonably good statistical probabilities that the credit card information could be still be intercepted by a malicious third party. Unfortunately, if this were to happen, the credit card information would still be in a plaintext format.

Thus, it can be used to engage in acts of credit card fraud, and worse yet, to conduct acts of identity theft, which could take the victim a long time to recover from. But not only does this credit card information have to be safe during the network transmission; it must also stay that way when it is stored in the database of the web application. For example, many databases still use insecure code, and thus are prime targets for any threat vector, namely that of SQL injection attacks. Probably the best way to secure against these forms of attack is to use what is known as encryption, which is a field of cryptography.

The basic point of encryption is to render the PII in a garbled state so that if it were to be intercepted by a cyberattacker, these datasets would be rendered useless unless the cyberattacker had the appropriate key to unlock them into a decipherable format. Thus, Chapter 2 reviewed the essential concepts of both encryption and cryptography and how they can used to secure the confidential information and data that are stored in the database of a web application and to make sure it stays that way while it is in transit across the network medium.

The topics covered in Chapter 2 included the following:

- An introduction to cryptography
- Message scrambling and descrambling
- Encryption and decryption
- Ciphertexts
- Symmetric key systems and asymmetric key systems
- The Caesar methodology
- Polyalphabetic encryption
- Block ciphers
- Initialization vectors
- Cipher block chaining
- Disadvantages of symmetric key cryptography
- The key distribution center
- Mathematical algorithms with symmetric cryptography
- The hashing function
- Asymmetric key cryptography
- Public keys and public private keys
- The differences between asymmetric and symmetric cryptography
- The disadvantages of asymmetric cryptography
- The mathematical algorithms of asymmetric cryptography
- The public key infrastructure
- The digital certificates

- How the public key infrastructure works
- Public key infrastructure policies and rules
- The LDAP protocol
- The public cryptography standards
- Parameters of public keys and private keys
- How many servers?
- Security policies
- Securing the public keys and the private keys
- Message digests and hashes
- Security vulnerabilities of hashes
- A technical review of cryptography
- The security of the DES
- Asymmetric and public key cryptography
- The RSA algorithm
- How to find large prime integers for the RSA algorithm
- The use of padding in the RSA algorithm
- Specific cyberattacks on the RSA algorithm
- The digital signature algorithm
- The elliptic curve digital signature algorithm
- The use of hash functions
- The security requirements of hash functions
- A technical overview of hash function algorithms
- The technical details of the secure hash algorithm SHA-1
- Key distribution centers
- The public key infrastructure and certificate authority

Just as it is important to secure the network lines of communications from the server that houses the web application to the device of the end user (and vice versa), as well as the PII that is transmitted across on it, it is equally important to examine the web application for both known and unknown vulnerabilities, weaknesses, and gaps. This is done through penetration testing and threat hunting, which were discussed in Chapter 3. There is one true way to determine how safe and imminently "hackable" your current web app or infrastructure is – and that is to have an objective third party conduct a penetration test.

The chapter began by illustrating the unknown flaws that may exist in web apps and infrastructures using true stories. We defined penetration testing as a real-world, simulated attack conducted by a certified and experienced engineer. We presented critical elements of penetration testing that need to be understood. We began this exposé by presenting the key types of penetration testing:

- External penetration testing
- Web application testing

- Internal penetration testing
- SSID or wireless testing
- Social engineering, including phishing and call campaigns
- Mobile application testing

We then defined the finding levels:

- Critical
- High
- Medium
- Low
- Informational

Next, we discussed the many frameworks and compliances that require penetration testing, such as:

- PCI
- HIPAA
- ISO 27001
- SOC 1/SOC 2
- FedRAMP
- NIST
- CIS
- COBIT
- HITRUST

We then introduced the reader to the very important OWASP organization and its Top Ten Web Application Flaws list, which included the following:

1. Injection
2. Broken authentication
3. Sensitive data exposure
4. XML external entities (XXE)
5. Broken access control
6. Security misconfiguration
7. Cross-site scripting (XSS)
8. Insecure deserialization
9. Using components with known vulnerabilities
10. Insufficient logging and monitoring

We then listed common tools for the pen tester's toolkit, followed by a detailed process for testing a web application. This process spanned several pages and introduced you to the thoroughness a good tester will employ.

We next suggested that excellence in the penetration test process will also involve the concepts of:

1. Intelligence gathering
2. Exploitation at a thorough level
3. Documentation that is professional, detailed, and helpful
4. Discussion of findings with the client in a helpful and informational way

Finally, we ended with a key takeaway that investment in annual penetration tests can save many dollars in fines, fees, and potential business loss.

Chapter 4 presented the criticality of threat hunting in an organization to keep applications, assets, PII, IP, and critical data safe. We learned that expert threat hunting can reduce hacker dwell time and lead to findings that just might save a business millions.

We covered:

- A ransomware scenario in a company that did not have preventative threat hunting
- Successful threat hunting narratives demonstrating successful threat discovery

We illustrated the reality of cyber threats through the aforementioned narratives, as well as presenting shocking but true information on nation-states and their cyberattack agendas. In particular, we:

- Presented China's 3 Rs and other key info from a recent FBI report
- Noted resources on the recent events in Iran
- Documented actual cyber occurrences recently visualized in a security operations center, underscoring the fact that Iran is trying to hack us

We then heard from an analyst on three types of threat hunting:

- Intelligence based
- Tools techniques and procedures based
- Trend based

Next, we reviewed the MITRE ATT&CK framework, a globally accessible knowledge base of bad actor tactics and techniques. We discussed common tools such as:

- EDR and MDR
- SIEM
- IDS
- The richness of an enhanced visibility window when the three tools are used together

We further concluded that although EDR technology is getting better and may be changing the SOC makeup, the SIEM still remains at the heart of MDR. We then reviewed the threat hunting process and the subsequent secondary search and correlation which can lead to more discoveries. We finished with the attributes of a good threat hunter, followed by resources in organizations geared to train and certify, such as SANS, ISACA and (ISC)[2].

We concluded that threat hunters and SOC services are *needed* – the threats are real, as demonstrated in the nation-state scenarios. Further, nation-states are involved in espionage and cyberattacks with the intent to acquire data, do harm, and further their initiatives.

Index

Page numbers in *italics* refer to figures.